PROVOKING MAGIC: LIGHTING OF INGO MAURER

PROVOKING
MAGIC
LIGHTING OF
INGO MAURER

Kim Hastreiter · Julie V. Iovine · Claude Maurer · Ingo Maurer

Smithsonian
Cooper-Hewitt, National Design Museum

(Cover)
L'Eclat Joyeux, 2005.
White European and
colored Chinese porcelain,
chopsticks, metal. One-off.

(Previous spread)
Birds Birds Birds, 1992.
Metal, goose-feather
wings, 24 low-voltage
bulbs, tin-plated metal
parts, cables.

CONTENTS

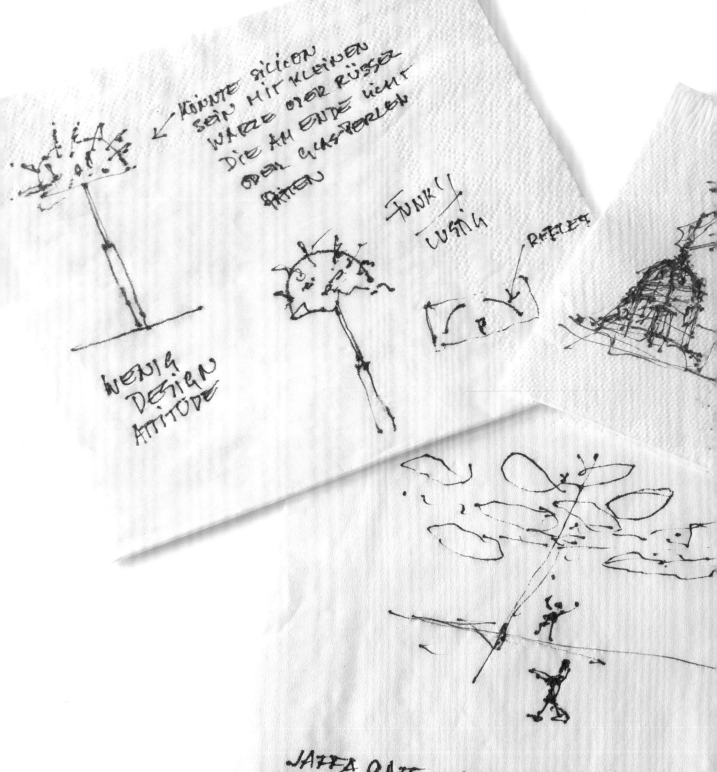

← Könnte silicon
sein mit kleinen
Warze oder Rüssel
die am ende licht
oder glasperlen
hätten

Funky /
lustig

REFLEX

Wenig
Design
Attitude

JAFFA GATE - JERUSALEM - SILVER
MOVES WITH THE WIND. MOBILE LIK
LIGHT REFLECTS ON THOUSAND OF SILVER

Sketches. Pen on paper napkin, 1994–2006.

Foreword

PAUL WARWICK THOMPSON

I first met Ingo Maurer in 1988, when, as a curator of contemporary design at the Design Museum in London, I selected his *YaYaHo* light for an exhibition. Twenty years later, I remain as enthralled by his work as I was then. It is with real pleasure that Cooper-Hewitt presents Ingo Maurer's first museum retrospective in America.

Ingo's audacious and theatrical installations at the Milan Furniture and Lighting Fair are always the star attraction of this annual design event. In a crowded, dark room, magical, glowing works are unveiled before a hungry press, and Ingo always stands in the center of the showroom like a bemused, benign magician. His shows are pure wizardry, with designers and students poring over light sources, scrutinizing circuitry, all eager to figure out how the magic has been conjured up.

To place Ingo Maurer in the stately setting of Cooper-Hewitt's Carnegie Mansion is truly exciting. The Mansion's somber interiors are the perfect foil and backdrop for Ingo's humor and technological tours de force. And to invoke the spirits of the Mansion's original residents, Andrew and Louise Carnegie, is so typical of Ingo's wicked humor. The contrast between the sobriety of the Carnegies and the bohemianism of Ingo Maurer could not be greater.

I wish to thank my old friend and museum colleague, Alexander von

7

Vegesack, Director of the Vitra Design
Museum, who played an important
role in the inception of this project; and
Barbara Bloemink, the Museum's former
Curatorial Director, who laid the foun-
dations for this exhibition with such
enthusiasm. I also thank Jocelyn Groom,
our Head of Exhibitions, Chul R. Kim,
Head of Publications, and our graphic
designers, Tsang Seymour Design,
for the invaluable role they played in
creating this exhibition and book.

I extend our gratitude to contributors
Kim Hastreiter and Julie Iovine for their
perspectives of writer and friend, which
each of them brings to this book. But
my particular thanks go to Ingo and
his team. We never could have realized
this exhibition and book without the
dedication and meticulous attention to
detail of Hagen Sczech, Ingo's daughter
Claude Maurer, Gabi Kümmerlin, and, of
course, Ingo himself.

Lastly, thanks are due to Erana Stennett
and Lex Fenwick of Bloomberg. They
were both quick to recognize the poetry
of Ingo Maurer's work and come forward as sponsors of this great New
York event.

FOREWORD

Sketches. Pen on paper
napkin, 1994–2006.

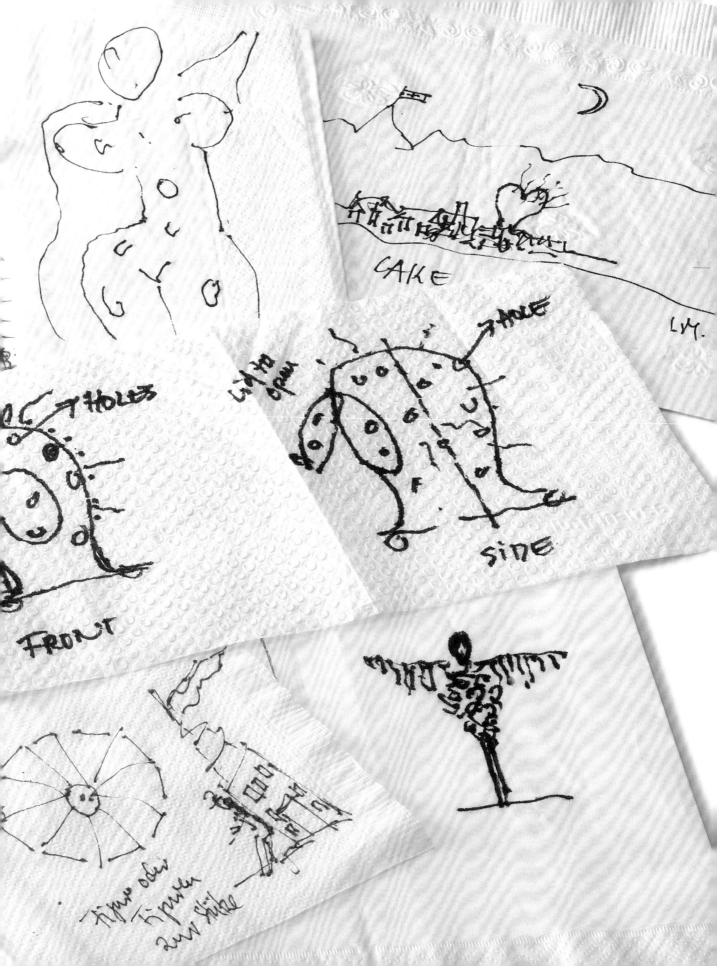

CAKE

LM.

7 HOLES

7 HOLE

LM to open

FRONT

SIDE

I met Ingo Maurer serendipitously
almost three decades ago, when I was
a young artist living in a loft off Canal
Street. He galloped into my life late
one dreary afternoon as I was hanging
out at home with a college friend
blasting music. I almost had a heart
attack when I answered the banging
on my door and saw this stranger who
looked like a movie star stride into
my loft. He bellowed "Hello" and intro-
duced himself as my new upstairs
neighbor. This tall, handsome man said
he was a lighting designer named
Ingo from Munich. He seemed beside
himself with excitement about his new
home-away-from-home, New York
City. "Look at it!" he cried, pointing
out my windows to the World Trade
Center towers on one side and the
Empire State Building on the other.
"It's beautiful! Look at the skyline,
look at all the people, look at the light!
New York is fantastic!" He had to
return to Munich that evening but told
me, "When I come back in a month
we will go salsa dancing!" It turned
out that Ingo did love to dance, but I
would soon learn that S.O.B.'s was just
the tip of the iceberg. From that day
on, whenever he arrived in town, he
would promptly come knocking at
my door to see what was up. I would
then drag him around with me to my
watering holes, crazy downtown clubs,
eccentric parties, drag performances,
art extravaganzas, and after-hour bars
that were my life in those days. His
enthusiasm was wild and his appetite

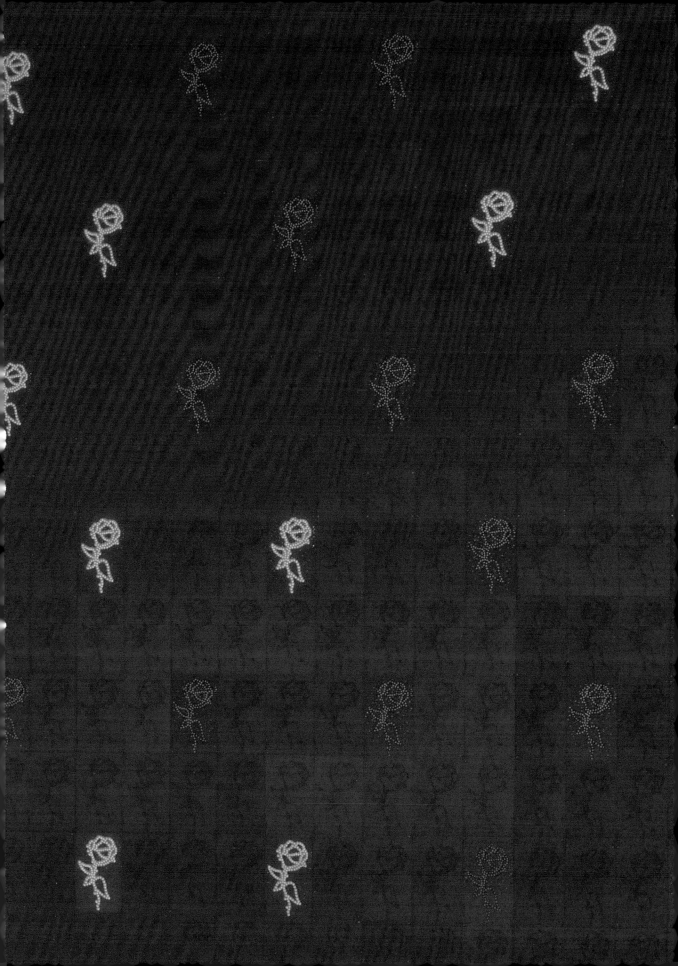

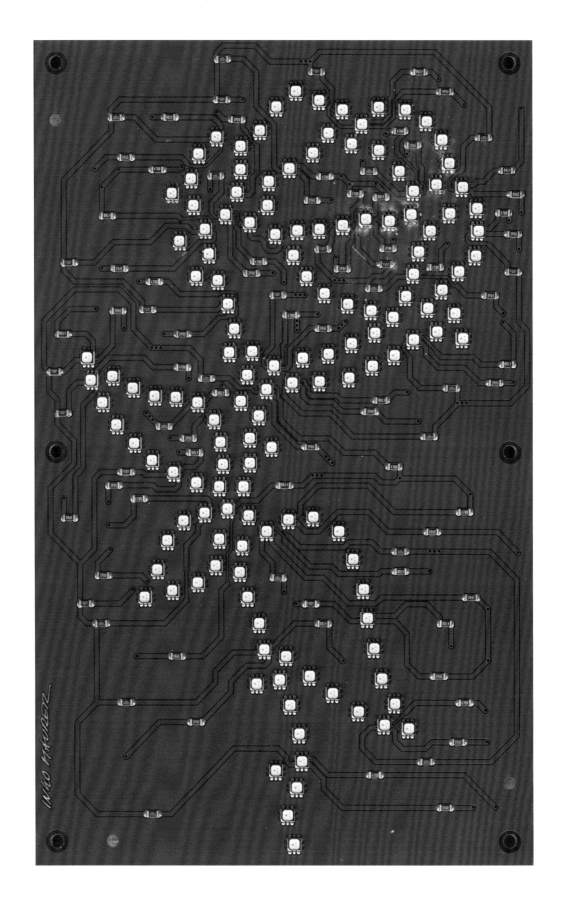

(Previous Spread)
Rose, Rose on the Wall,
2006. Red circuit boards,
RGB-LEDs, wood, steel.
Custom-made object.

**Arrangement with
OLED Coffee Table**.
Glass, organic LEDs,
steel, and two armchairs
by Jean Prouvé.

(Opposite)
Rose, Rose on the Wall
(detail).

Maurer is fascinated by the
aesthetics of circuit boards
and other technical components. He was the first to
reveal their unique charm
and beauty, when he started
working with LED technol-
ogy in 1997. Before that,
LEDs were not employed
for interior lighting.

*Johannes
let's do
a cerceuit board
in clear!*

was voracious for all the fun cultural insanity that used to define downtown New York. We not only became fast friends, but my friends became his friends, and vice versa. For years we cheered each other on as both of our very different careers evolved. He became a fan of my magazine, and I began collecting his lights.

Almost thirty years have passed and Ingo, his wonderful wife Jenny, and his extended family of kids, grandkids, friends, and coworkers are still family to me. How lucky and proud we New Yorkers should be to have Ingo creating this show of his amazing work at Cooper-Hewitt, in his favorite city in the world! Although I am not a design historian or scholar, I was thrilled to be asked to put together this little snapshot of my unique, brilliant, and dear friend. He is not only a beautiful, spirited artist and a designer of light that has often been compared to poetry, but he is a rare bird in the world of design—bringing humanity, humility, humor, and a great big gigantic sparkle to a field that sometimes feel dry, pretentious, and ultra-serious. Bravo, my friend!

13

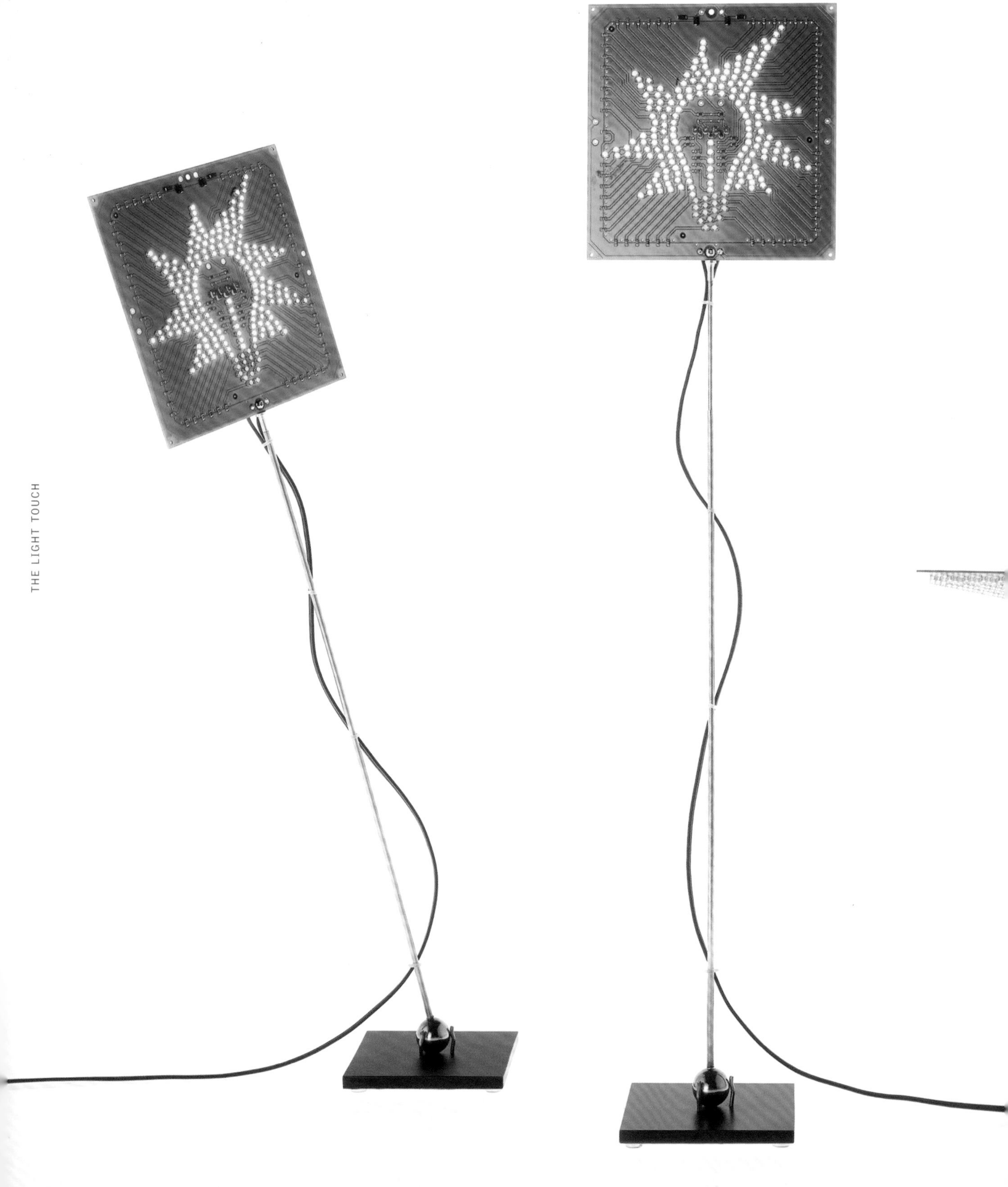

Flora Dee, 2001.
Circuit board, LEDs,
stainless steel, metal.

EL.E.Dee, 2001.
Circuit board, LEDs,
stainless steel, metal.

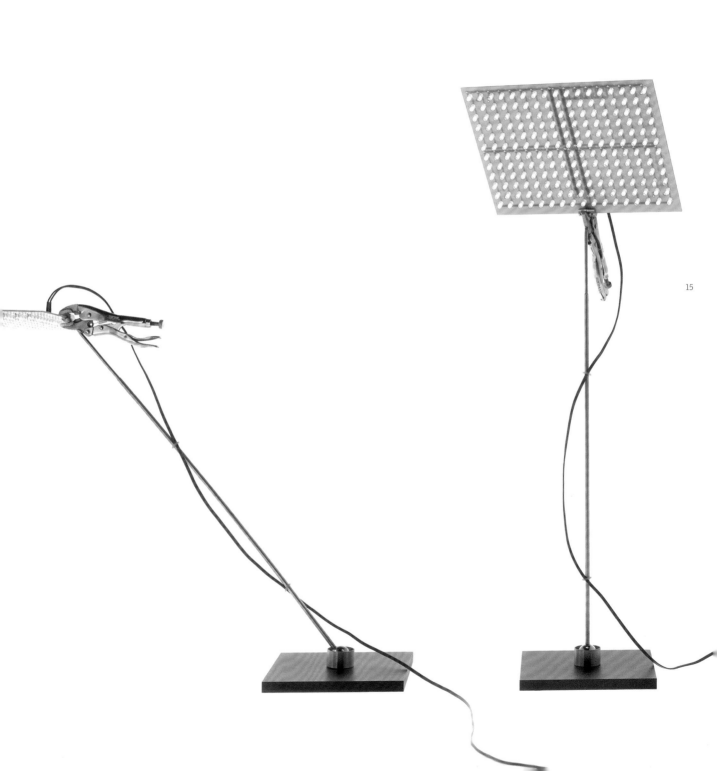

15

Licht.Enstein, 2001.
Plexiglas, circuit boards,
steel. One-off.

THE LIGHT BULB

KH: You have always been intrigued
by the light bulb as a design object and
invention, and have used it as a continual inspiration within your design. When
did your "light bulb go on" about your
very first light bulb–inspired design?

IM: Years ago I was lying on my back
in a very cheap hotel room in Venice.
I'd had a great lunch and a whole bottle
of wine to myself. I looked up at this
15-watt light bulb on the ceiling and fell
in love with it. I remember thinking,
What a combination! This is the shape
of poetry and industry—a fantastic
marriage between the two.

KH: Do you think the light bulb will
ever become extinct? How do you see
its evolution?

IM: I think that it will take a while to
wean ourselves off this bulb. But, envi-
ronmentally, it is very important that we
do. We are using too much electricity.

KH: What about these compact fluo-
rescent light bulbs? Environmentalists
love them, but the light they give off
is so ugly.

IM: My big argument against them is
that their light has no feeling. They are
absolutely depressing and bad for your
mental health!

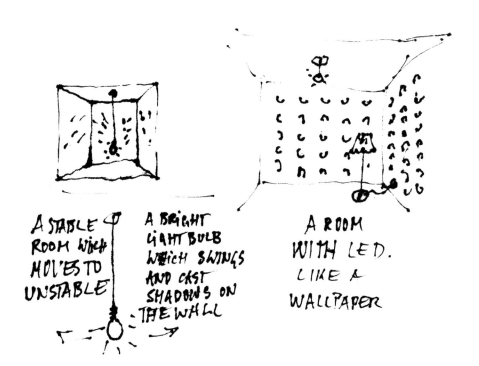

A STABLE ROOM WHICH MOVES TO UNSTABLE

A BRIGHT LIGHTBULB WHICH SWINGS AND CAST SHADOWS ON THE WALL

A ROOM WITH LED. LIKE A WALLPAPER

Sketch. Pen on paper, 2001.

Swinging Bulb (schwingende Glühbirne). Play with shadow, light, and a heart (detail), 2001. Lightbulb, wood. Installation.

The shadow completes the form of the heart when swinging to and fro.

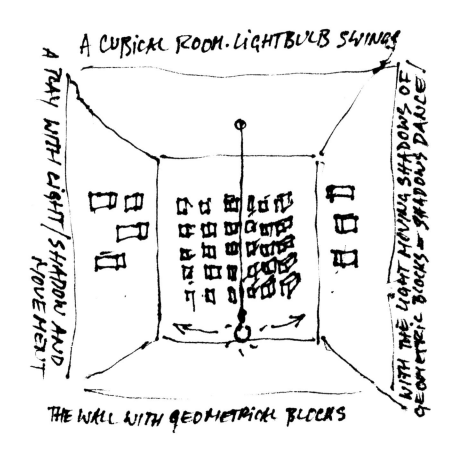

A CUBICAL ROOM. LIGHTBULB SWINGS

A PLAY WITH LIGHT/SHADOW AND MOVEMENT

WITH THE LIGHT MOVING SHADOWS OF GEOMETRIC BLOCKS = SHADOWS DANCE!

THE WALL WITH GEOMETRICAL BLOCKS

Flying bulbs, 1993.

KH: But the melting polar icecaps are depressing, too. What are we going to do? What are you going to do?

IM: We are working on something called OLED (Organic Light-Emitting Diodes), which we think could be the future. It does not yet give off a bright enough light, but we are working on it.

KH: Will a solution ever come in the form of a single bulb?

IM: No. We have to go in a different direction, such as developing walls or even wallpaper that lights up with LED.

21

ON FIRE

KH: If you were living before electricity, what kind of lights would you make?

IM: Fire! I am very fascinated by fire. I am now doing something with fire as part of a show in a huge castle in Milan. When they asked me to do it, I was hesitant, because I thought it would be such a vanity show, but I decided to make something outside, along the 200-meter façade, which spelled out the words "What the hell am I doing here?" The words will be on fire and burn all night long! Yes, it is really crazy. And yes, it really will say "What the hell am I doing here?"

KH: Speaking of fire, I know you love that insane festival, Burning Man. Why on Earth would you want to schlep to the Nevada desert in high summer in 120-degree heat and sleep outdoors?

IM: (laughing) Well, because I am burning! I go to Burning Man because, first of all, the nature attracts me. I love the desert. Also, it is the best event for me in the world because I see highly creative people who create sometimes very junky but also very good things. Nobody makes any demands on you to "Look at me!" and no one judges you. It is really straight from your heart, your brain, or your feet. All the people are sharing everything with you and everybody is really part of it. It is a big community of thirty thousand people and it has this enormous energy.

KH: Do they really burn stuff there, even in all that heat?

IM: Yes! People have built palaces and then set fires to them. But this is what brings people together emotionally. It is wonderful. I have met American friends who said, "This is where we fill our tanks for the rest of the year." You have to be creative there. And then the fire...it is so archaic.

DESIGN FOR EVERYONE

KH: You are an egalitarian. For as long as I have known you, I have seen

Johnny B. Good, 2002.
Designers: Ingo Maurer,
Bernhard Dessecker.
Glass, Teflon, plastic.

Holonzki, 2000.
Designers: Ingo Maurer,
Eckard Knuth.
Glass hologram, metal.

how you love meeting and talking to all sorts of people, and you are not at all judgmental. I have seen you get a greater thrill from an interesting taxi driver or a waiter in a coffee shop than with a sophisticated artist or socialite. Does it bother you that some of these regular people cannot afford to own your work?

IM: Yes, it does bother me.

KH: Wouldn't you want to make a light that costs $30 that everyone could buy?

IM: Yes! I would love to create something really sophisticated, functional, and which gives joy. Unfortunately, I live in a town which is really expensive, and I do not want to go to China, produce it cheaply, and sell it here. I have been trying, and I will keep on trying.

THE ANTIMATERIALIST WHO MAKES STUFF

KH: You are one of the least materialistic people that I can think of. You really and truly do not give a hoot about possessions or money. Were you always this way? Were your parents like this?

IM: My parents were not materialistic at all. I was raised as a Catholic, but my father was very much into Buddhism and Far Eastern philosophy. Less was

aR-ingo, 1984. Designers: Ron Arad, Ingo Maurer. Aluminum in honeycomb structure, steel.

more. We lived an extremely simple life. This simplicity was one of the great things I inherited from my parents.

KH: How can someone that does not really care about stuff build a business based around selling stuff?

IM: (Laughs) I guess I had an urge to create, and it happened by chance. I had this impression about this funny little light bulb in Venice and I had a family to feed. I began by playing, and then of course the whole thing with the lights started to get out of hand.

KH: And then you had employees to feed.

27

IM: Yes, then I had Gloria Capitola, one of my first secretaries! I think it was a fake name. We sat in a basement with wood shavings, packaging, and invoices.

KH: You sometimes seem less interested in designing products or "things" than in designing an experience to share with people. How do you think function plays into your list of priorities?

IM: Function is extremely important to me. Even if I make a joke, when you look at my designs, they are functional and they make good light.

KH: Do you think that, if you did not have to feed all these people in your company, you would do more experiential design? What I see you get the most excited by are experiences you have created for the public. Your legendary "happenings" or your public works—like the huge snowflake over Fifth Avenue, or making dry-ice smoke under a bridge in a canal, or suspending thousands of candles in an old, run-down theater in Harlem—seem to thrill you most of all.

IM: It is always a joy for me when we create a "happening," when people feel emotionally touched. When people walk through the huge fair in Milan, they come to our stand after seeing a thousand booths and a smile comes to their lips or their eyes. It is a big reward for me.

REFLECTING ON REFLECTION

KH: Reflection is another of your great creative inspirations. You always speak about the way light reflects off this or that—whether it is sparkling on water or wafting around smoke or bouncing off a disco ball. Why does reflection appeal to you so much? Is this because it plays with infinity in a way, or is it because it is mysterious?

IM: I think it is mysterious, because light travels so incredibly fast in so many different ways that you never

minimalism has become a style! For me it is still an attitude.

Part of BakaRú lighting system, 1986. Plastic, metal, ceramic, Multi-Mirror reflectors with protective glass cover.

really know where it comes from.
I like that very, very much.

KH: What are some of the most signifi-
cant examples of reflection that you
have seen in your life?

IM: The most incredible is when I see
wind blow through the olive trees and
you can see that the leaves have a dark
side and a light side. I like very much
to watch light moving, especially light
or wind on water. I have watched fish-
ermen on the lake many times. Sitting,
daydreaming, watching the sun jump-
ing from one little wave to the other—
you get into a kind of delirium, it
is hypnotic.

HE LOVES NEW YORK

KH: If you could live in one city instead
of Munich, what would it be?

IM: New York, definitely! When you are
in love, you just have that feeling for
it. It is really wonderful to see so many
beautiful and mixed faces, different
colors and smells. I love the energy. I
love looking out of my window at the
sky, which at times looks like a Turner
painting! America has been the best
thing to happen to me in my life.

KH: Everything seems so bad in America
as of late. I often think, How can people
still love us when we act so badly?

Lampampe, 1980.
Japanese paper, metal.

IM: Well, because you have a lot of wonderful people here. You have a lot of super artists, great films, fantastic theater. To me, the human beings are what make New York so fascinating.

KH: You make a beautiful public mark on New York every winter, when your enormous crystal snowflake goes up over Fifth Avenue and Fifty-seventh Street. Have you ever wanted to make any other types of public light in other neighborhoods? I remember sitting with you in a daze on September 11th six years ago, staring at the strange rescue lights playing off the smoke and fire pouring out of Ground Zero. We were so sad. What did you think of the "towers of light" commemoration when it first went up?

IM: I was moved. I have to tell you one thing that put me in tears. Two years ago, on September 11th, I was having a drink with some friends at about midnight on Church Street, and as I walked home, I looked up at the towers of light (which are turned on every year on that day) and saw what I thought were thousands of pieces of paper swirling around inside the tall columns. Suddenly, I realized it was not paper but *birds*—I mean *thousands* of birds flying around frantically, as if they were trapped within those towers of light. It was incredible. It was one of the most astonishing things I have ever seen.

KH: I know. I saw it because you called me that night and woke me up shouting from the street for me to run to my window and look. It was an amazing and spooky sight to see. I remember we decided those birds were like the souls of the people who had died. It must have great meaning to you to open this amazing exhibit at Cooper-Hewitt in your favorite city in the month of September. The towers will likely still be lit when your show opens.

IM: Yes, but this show is definitely not looking backward. I look ahead and I enjoy every day.

Oh Mei Ma Weiss, 2005. Metal, glass, six sheets of aluminum with white paint coat.

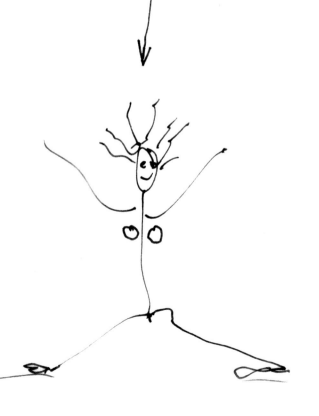

THE NAME OF AN EGYPTIAN GIRL I KNOW.

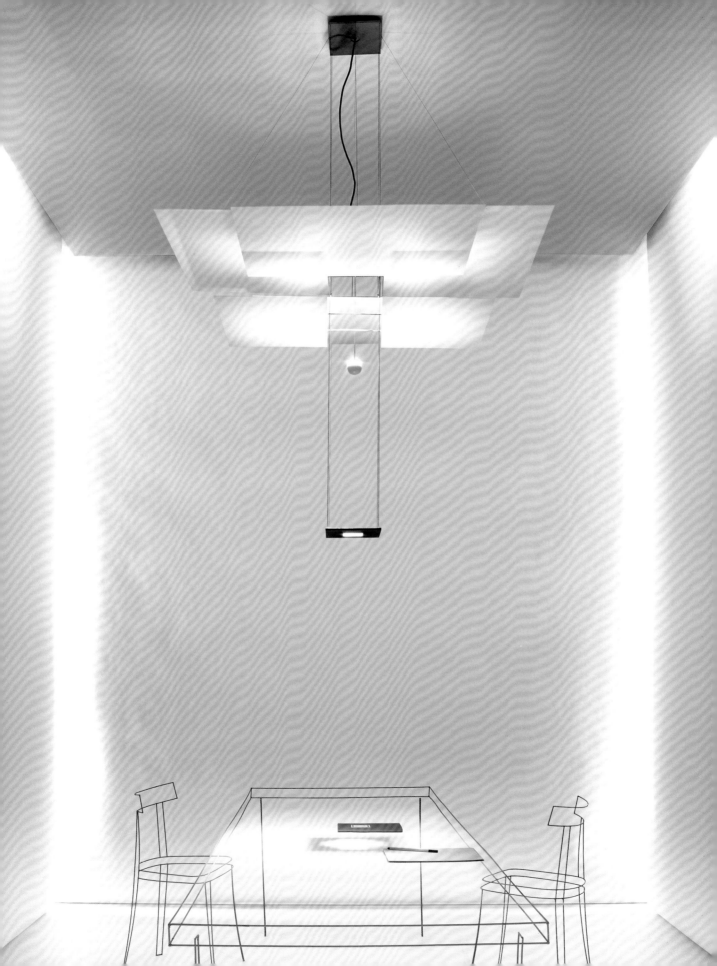

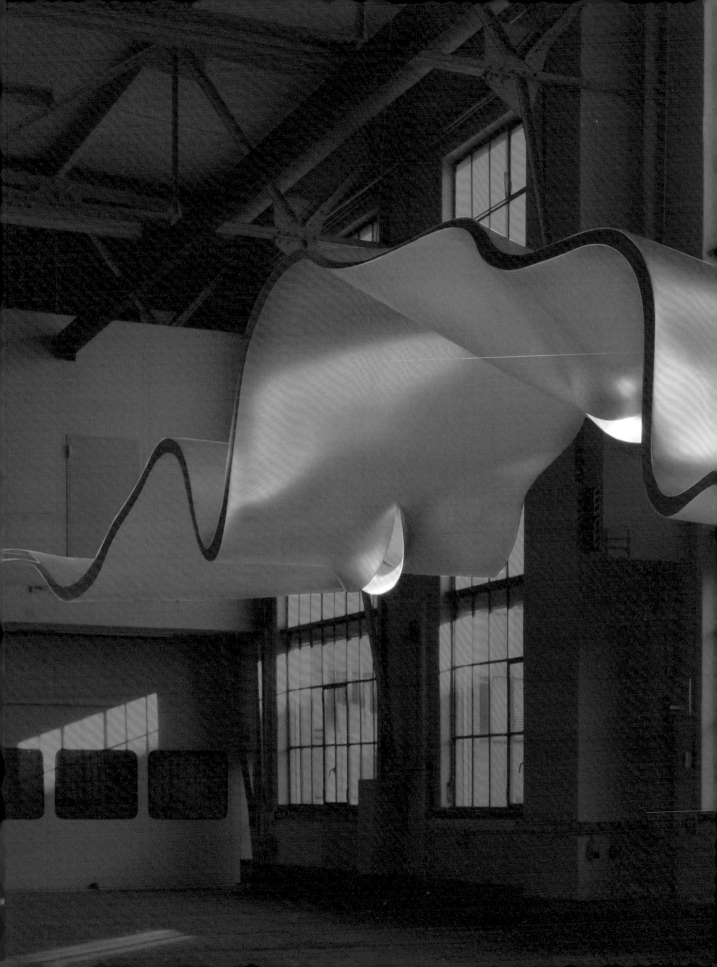

Illuminating with Memory and Emotion

Julie V. Iovine

It is no surprise that a light bulb with wings has turned out to be Ingo Maurer's signature design. The seventy-five-year-old designer is truly a *rara avis*: part designer, part artist, part entrepreneur and magician, whose work defies easy categorization. His career spans more than forty years of risk-taking as a technical innovator, shrewd manufacturer, and inspired dreamer.

Although he was born in southern Germany and has always maintained his work base in Munich, the words "German designer" do not work for Maurer. They suggest instead someone like Dieter Rams. An exact contemporary and also a revered designer, Rams was raised on Bauhaus principles of form, function, and no messing around for effect, whose efficient industrial design systems are rigorously pragmatic and precisely ordered, as one might expect from a German designer.

Such words, though true enough, simply do not conjure the hippie-haired man with his sneakers and slightly manic blue-eyed gaze and 100-watt charisma as he strides around one of his installations—perhaps a tunnel in Cologne where masked bicyclists carrying illuminated fish dart through a dry-ice fog, or an abandoned theater in Harlem where a swarm of flickering

Golden Ribbon, 2005.
Aluminum, gold leaf
Custom-made object.

Ingo Maurer started to
design Golden Ribbon in
1994. Each one is custom-
made for the particular
space. Maurer forms the
lead model by hand. Under
the supervision of a team
member, the two layers
of aluminum are bent and
formed in a metal work-
shop; gold leaf is then
applied manually.

37

One from the Heart, 1989.
Plastic, metal, adjustable
glass mirror.

**Sketch for a vase
for Salviati**, 2001.
Pen on paper.

Cuore Aperto, 1996.
Aluminum, steel, light
bulbs, goose-feather
wings. One-off.

candles float over a reflecting pool
splattered with cooling drips of wax.
Nor do they muster the uncompro-
mising perfectionist deciding on the
day before the opening of the Tel Aviv
Performing Arts Center (designed in
1994 with longtime collaborator and
friend Ron Arad) to swap out a chandelier that took him a year to design
for a bare light bulb in the foyer.

Trying to classify Maurer is less mean-
ingful than trying to figure out what
makes him tick, and how his lighting
designs have managed to illuminate
needs we did not even know we had.

Born in 1932, Maurer grew up during
the mounting madness of World War II,
but he was also relatively far removed,
on Lake Constance, near the German-
Swiss border. His father was a fisher-
man and inventor: a ham smoker, he
devised what became a profitable
patent for the family. But it was boat-
ing on the lake and observing the
endless ballet of light on water that
gave him his first sense of the power
of light—what he would later call,
in a rare moment of dense German-
speak, a "psychoactive material."

Rather than the controlled restraint
of Germanic modernism, Maurer seems
to spring from an earlier German tra-
dition of romanticism and the legacy of
Karl Friedrich Schinkel, Ludwig van
Beethoven, and Johann Wolfgang von
Goethe, himself an early interpreter
of the subjective nature of color and
refraction, whose last words, famously,
were "Mehr licht (More light)!"

Kokoro sketch, 1996.
Ink and pencil on paper.

Kokoro, 1998. Designers:
Dagmar Mombach,
Ingo Maurer and Team.
Japanese paper, metal,
stainless steel, glass,
adjustable glass mirror.

Kokoro (detail).

**Paper rolls for
MaMo Nouchies**.

43

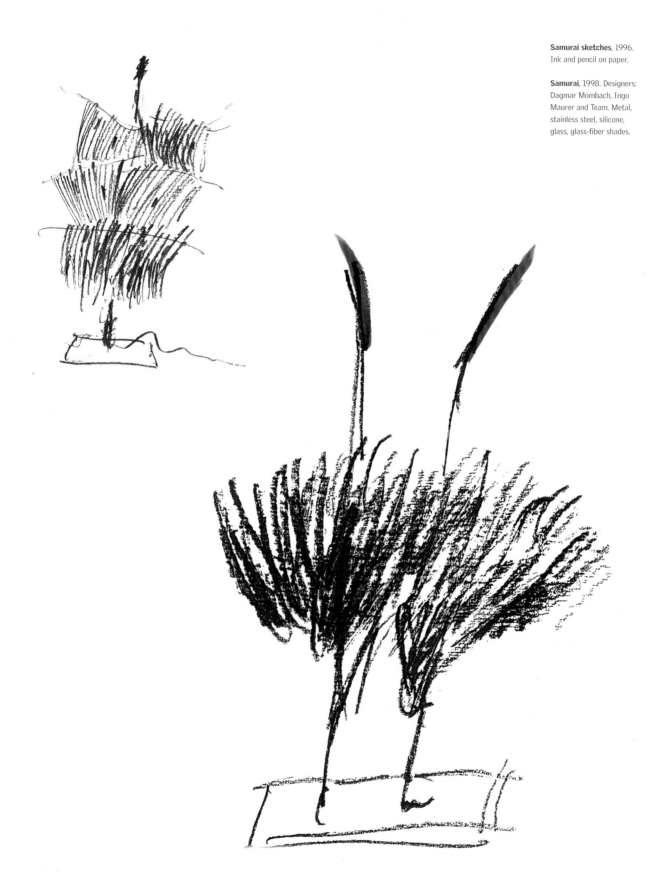

Samurai sketches, 1996. Ink and pencil on paper.

Samurai, 1998. Designers: Dagmar Mombach, Ingo Maurer and Team. Metal, stainless steel, silicone, glass, glass-fiber shades.

Bulb, 1966. Hand-blown
crystal glass, polished
chromium-plated metal,
top-chromated bulb.

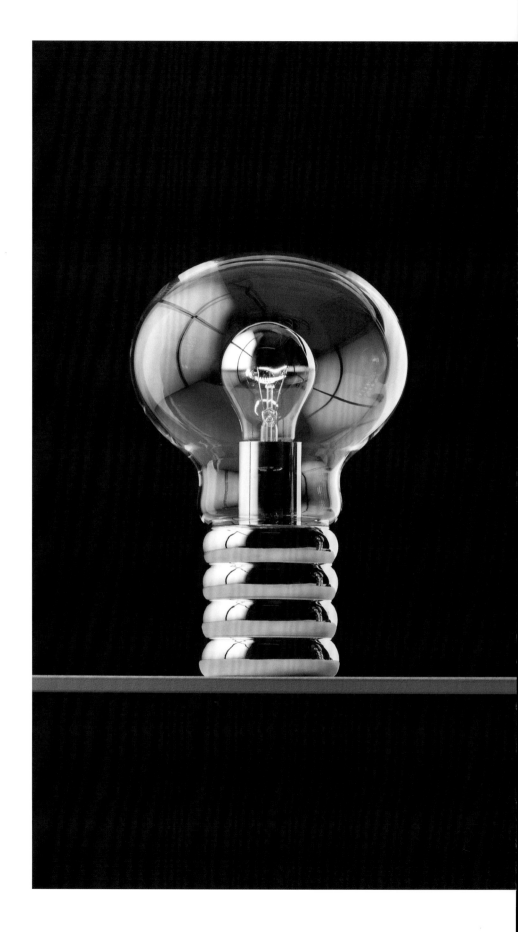

The romantic strain that runs through Maurer's work is not restricted to the explicit shapes appearing in such lamps as the 1989 *One from the Heart* (a tribute to the Francis Ford Coppola film of the same name); the 1994 *One for the Recession* (heart folded); or the pulsating three-dimensional paper heart of the 1998 *Kokoro*. There is optimism saturated with mystical glee—the recurrent theme of candles, a gold-leafed light sculpture in the shape of a ribbon caught in mid-flutter from a Baroque altarpiece, all that red—suggesting both the Catholicism of his village childhood and an unquenchable hopefulness. Entirely absent from his work is any hint of that contemporary crutch, irony. Maurer's uncynical version of modernism seems somehow at once more innocent and more forward-looking.

Maurer works memory and emotion into his designs as another might use wire and glue. His first notable light, *Bulb* (1966), is pure icon: a glass bulb inside a gigantic glass bulb. The idea came to him all of a sudden as a kind of vision, he says, when he was stretched on a mattress in a cheap pension in Venice, staring up at the bare fixture in the ceiling and remembering a similar bulb his father had hung in a window. *Bulb*, which Maurer, thinking no one else would take it seriously, manufactured himself, was almost immediately added to the design collection of The Museum of Modern Art. A later design, *Porca Miseria!* (1994), is more overtly loaded with emotion. An explosion of crockery charged with the euphoria of released energy, it is one of several designs that originated as a wedding present for friends.

For Maurer, it is rarely enough to make an impact. He wants people to interact with his designs, and many are incomplete without that interaction. *Zettel'Z* is a bristling sunburst of wires tipped with clips and sheets of white paper, which, in the sales catalog, comes with a hand-scrawled message from Maurer: "These lamps need a co-designer with fantasy and patience." Other lamps involve adjustable reflector mirrors, wires, or counterweights, all to force users to get involved, to join in being keepers of the flame. The *YaYaHo*, Maurer's most imitated work, has some 276 components ready to be customized.

Like a true poet, Maurer treats light as the ultimate found object. In the spirit of Italian designer Achille Castiglioni, his lamps often assemble a magpie collection of ad-hoc materials gathered through the designer's travels, both far-flung and very close to home. Helmut Bauer, the curator of the first exhibition of Maurer's work in Germany, at the Museum Villa Stuck, Munich, in 1992, described him as making "his way around the world accumulating nothing but new ideas for lighting." Goose feathers, tea strainers, and porcelain dolls have all been brought into play. *Bibibibi* (1982), topped with a broad-brimmed shade and a feather, stands on red plastic chicken legs that Maurer stole from a Woolworth's store (a clerk would not sell him the broken merchandise).

The materials may be junk, but the underlying attitude is a serious appreciation for craft, and even his most seemingly industrial products, such

L'Eclat Joyeux, 2005.
White European and
colored Chinese porcelain,
chopsticks, metal. One-off.

Porca Miseria!,
1994. White European
porcelain, silverware,
metal. Limited edition.

Ingo Maurer working on
a special version of Porca
Miseria!, 2007.

as *Max.Mover*, with its telescoping
arm, are often laboriously assembled
by hand in on-site workshops. In
the early 1970s, Maurer supported
twenty-one Japanese artisans for
a year on Shikoku Island while they
made his *Uchida* lamps from traditional paper fans. The *MaMo Nouchies*
lamps, also made of Japanese paper,
require an eight-day process, adapted
from traditional dying techniques,
and involving soaking the papers, bind-
ing them by hand with thread, and
drying—skills that took years to perfect. Maurer's attraction to traditional
methods and low-tech materials
should not to be confused with a lack
of technical sophistication.

Maurer has conducted life as an
artist, living large and doing what
free spirits do—making soul-clearing
pilgrimages to the Egyptian desert,
attending Burning Man festivals—
but none of that has gotten in the
way of making his work both exquis-
itely refined and technologically
advanced. Deyan Sudjic, Director of
the Design Museum in London, cap-
tured that dual spirit when he
described Maurer's lights as "totems
of high-tech tribal culture."

Maurer has always stayed ahead
of the curve in terms of lighting innovations, and no one has made more
creative use of halogen lights. It took
three years to develop the low-voltage
halogen system of double cables that
makes *YaYaHo* work, and the experience almost bankrupted the company
before Maurer succeeded in introduc-
ing it in 1984. Compelled by his drive

Bibibibi, 1982. Porcelain,
metal, plastic.

YaYaHo, Elements
4 + 5, 1984. Porcelain,
glass, plastic, metal.

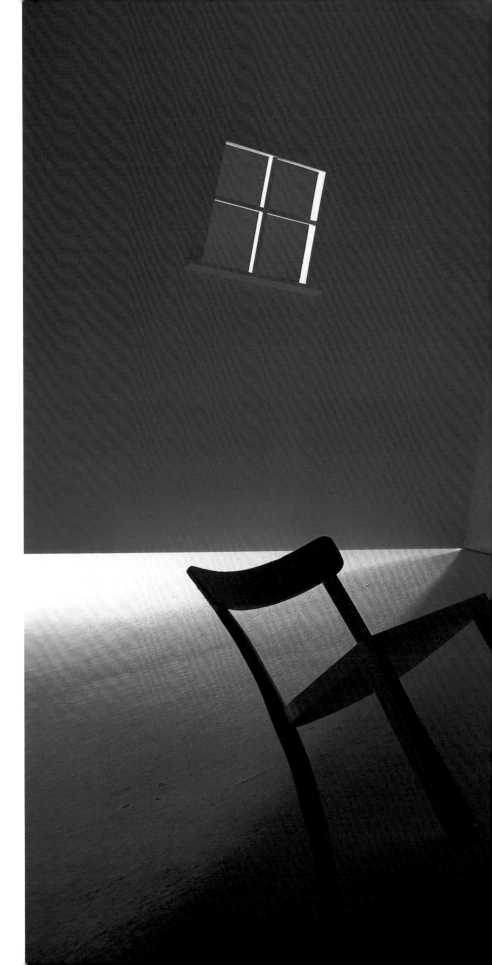

Wo bist du, Edison,...?,
1997. Acrylic glass,
aluminum, hologram 360°.

The hanging bulb and
socket are integrated
with a container shaped
after the profile of Thomas
Edison. The hologram is
the large, clear cylinder
showing the bulb.

to reduce lights to their most essential existence, Maurer, with the help
of engineer Hermann Kovacs, developed the *TouchTronic* in 1986, a
touch-triggered dimming switch that
works off the conductivity of the
human body. "Ingo has been ahead
of his time for forty years," says
Murray Moss of Moss in SoHo and
a dedicated champion of the designer.
"His work is not associated with
any one technology, he works with
them all. Inspired by Edison, he
has been brave enough to let even
the light bulb go out of his work."

Indeed, he made a hologram chandelier, *Wo bist du Edison,...?* (1997),
which is but the shadow of Edison's
invention like an apparition of Obi-Wan
Kenobi (actually conjured from more
than 2,600 separate images), and,
more recently, a number of ingenious
LED works. *Luster* (2004), for instance,
is a suspended sheet of glass bearing
the cartoon sketch of a chandelier
which magically twinkles with bursts
of LED light, but with no electrical
feed, thanks to a new conductive gel
sandwiched into the glass.

Creator, designer, manufacturer, and
packager, Maurer has from the begin-
ning controlled his message to an
extent few others have ever dared.
His creative team, which he calls "the
designery," now numbers more than
sixty people working in a converted
laundry building on Kaiserstrasse,
in a bohemian-friendly neighborhood
of Munich, not far from the walk-
up where he made his first *Bulb*. He
has said that he became his own

ILLUMINATING WITH MEMORY AND EMOTION

Symphonia Silenziosa
(detail), first installed in
the Louisiana Museum of
Modern Art, Copenhagen,
Denmark, 1996.

(Next spread)
Symphonia Silenziosa,
Vitra Design Museum,
2002. Installation using
parts of YaYaHo lighting
system and custom-made
paper sheets. Porcelain,
cable, paper, glass, plastic, metal.

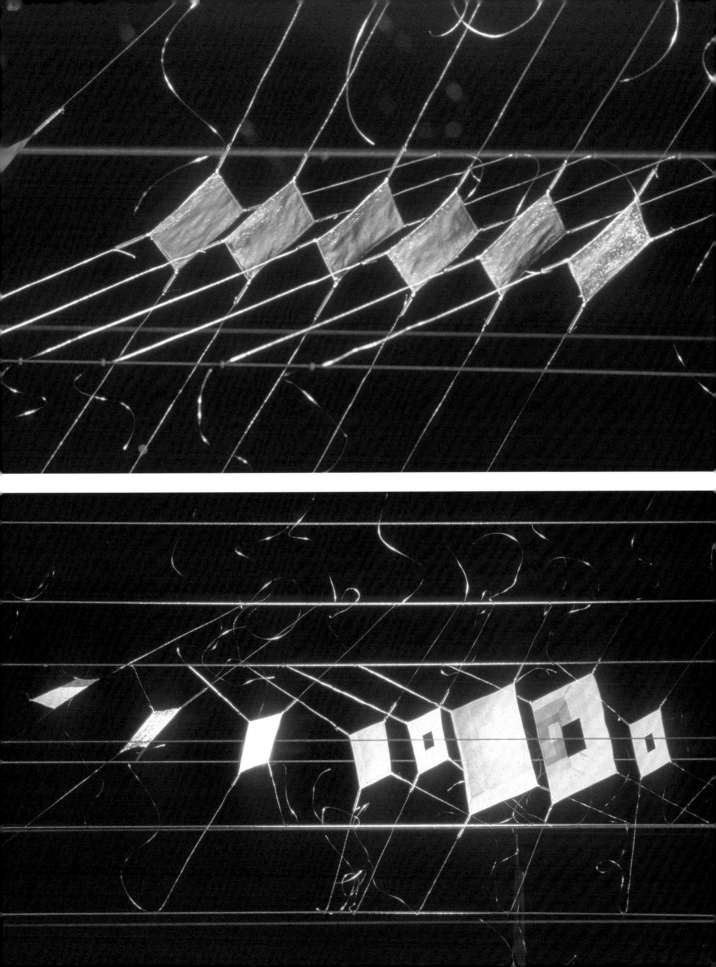

Lucellino, wall version, 1992. Glass, brass, plastic, handcrafted goose-feather wings.

manufacturer out of fear that his work would not measure up; in fact, it was an incredibly shrewd business move that took advantage of a tremendous upswing in German interest in contemporary design from the 1970s forward. From that time until nearly the present (when Americans took the torch), German shoppers were by far the largest importers of Italian design in the world, according to George Baylerian, founder of Material Connexion and a veteran of the international design scene. Maurer has always been a closet Italian; he speaks Italian as fluently as German. And his reputation and his designs quickly spread to Italy through highly developed German distribution routes. "He was able to live the life of an artist and still have an immediate market," Baylerian states. "And no less important is the fact that people will take risks when it comes to buying something the size of a lamp. And Maurer had the bold lamps to deliver."

Art installations have taken an increasingly important role in Maurer's life and work. "I am interested in turning an ordinary project into a kind of dream, an illusion," he told a reporter for *Metropolis* magazine in March 2007. Installation work has always been a key source not only for his own designs, but also for an entire generation of young designers coming through the ranks that he has both inspired and encouraged. For years his installations—happenings, really—have attracted thousands at the annual furniture fairs in Cologne and Milan, where Maurer has collaborated with

Ron Arad or sponsored works by such up-and-coming talents as Paul Cocksedge, who was named the 2004 Designer of the Year by the Design Museum, London.

Like the bulb in the Venetian pension which inspired his first light, Maurer seems to work in visions, sometimes encountered spontaneously—bulbs soldered to a power cord for a street festival in Haiti inspired *YaYaHo*—but just as often of his own making. *Lucellino*, the signature bulb which sprouts feathers, was first conceived for the show *Day and Night* at the Fondation Cartier in 1989, where a flock of them darted from the dusty dark of an abandoned war bunker. Similarly, a version of the gently wafting sheets of layered silver leaf that evolved into *Oh Mei Ma* originally appeared at a 1999 Issey Miyake fashion show in London.

Some Maurer events achieve the level of theatrical performance, such as the Fellini-esque circus of illuminated fish and bicyclists he staged on a footbridge over the Rhine one bitter-cold January in Cologne (thoughtfully providing hot soup at the end). His work was included alongside that of Sol LeWitt and Richard Serra in a public-arts program created for the Pearson International Airport in Toronto in 2004. But even his less rarified work, such as the gigantic steel domes, lacquered on the inside in primary colors, he made for the Munich subway station, casts a transfiguring aura of art in the dingiest settings.

Lucellino, table version, 1992. Glass, brass, plastic, handcrafted goose-feather wings.

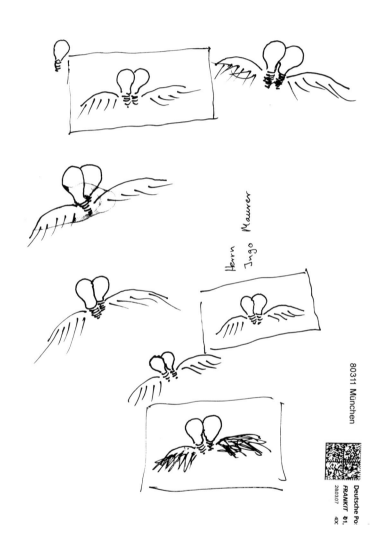

Winged bulbs embracing, sketches, 2007. Pen on paper.

It comes as little surprise that lighting programs at industrial-design schools do not claim Ingo Maurer as one of their own. He functions less like an industrial designer and more like an Alexander Calder or, perhaps, even a Martha Graham—a category unto himself whose poetic meter is measured in watts. He has understood well that, in the modern world, function has come to mean more than working parts, and that emotional resonance is equally essential. Above all, Maurer treats light as a dimensional object which, in his hands at least, will not only illuminate what we see, but change how we look at things.

65

Birdie, 2002.
Metal, goose-feather
wings, 12 low-voltage
bulbs, tin-plated metal
parts, cables.

Notes on Inspiration

Claude Maurer with Ingo Maurer

Until now, reflections on Ingo Maurer's work have appeared mainly in the pages of international interior-design magazines, often in interviews.

One question that has come up repeatedly is, Where does Ingo get his inspiration for his designs? Some ideas that have evolved into products have a story behind them; but for the most part the origin of his inspiration is difficult to pin down. This is a nebulous area where various elements collide, more an unfathomable maze than a description you could find in a manual. Nevertheless, I will try, in collaboration with my father, to explore this subject here. Who knows if we will reach a conclusion?

I think there are perhaps two paths to answering the question: One takes the reader on a zigzag journey to the center of the labyrinth, offering fleeting glimpses here and there, if not the full view of the source. The other is a more direct route, yet one that likely yields similar dissatisfaction.

An answer may come in the form of a quotation:

"The artist is a receptacle for emotions that come from all over the place: from the sky, from the earth, from a scrap of paper, from a passing shape, from a spider's web."[1]

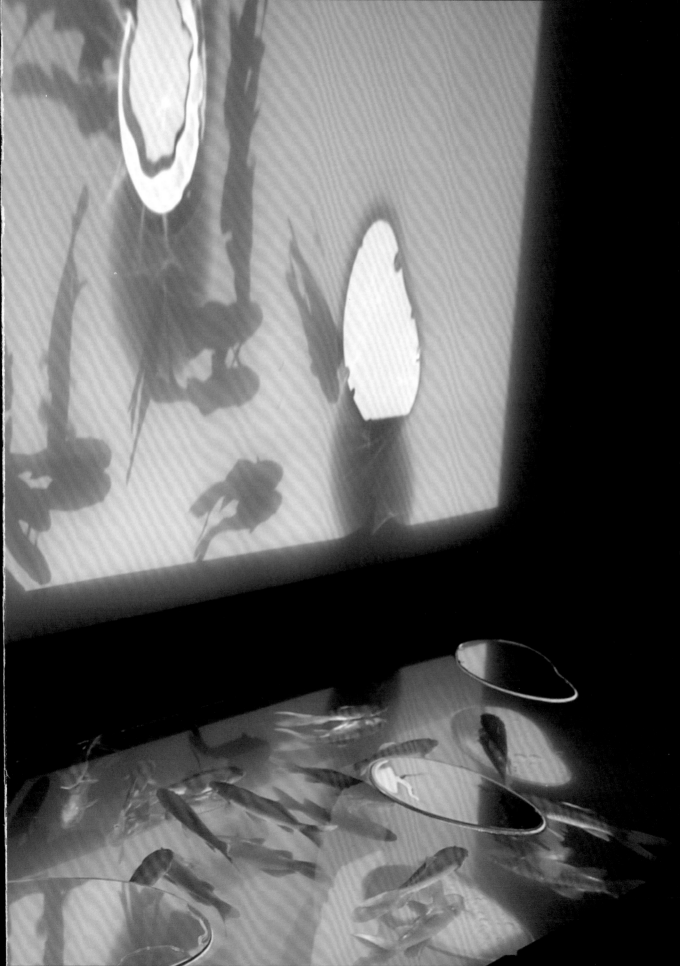

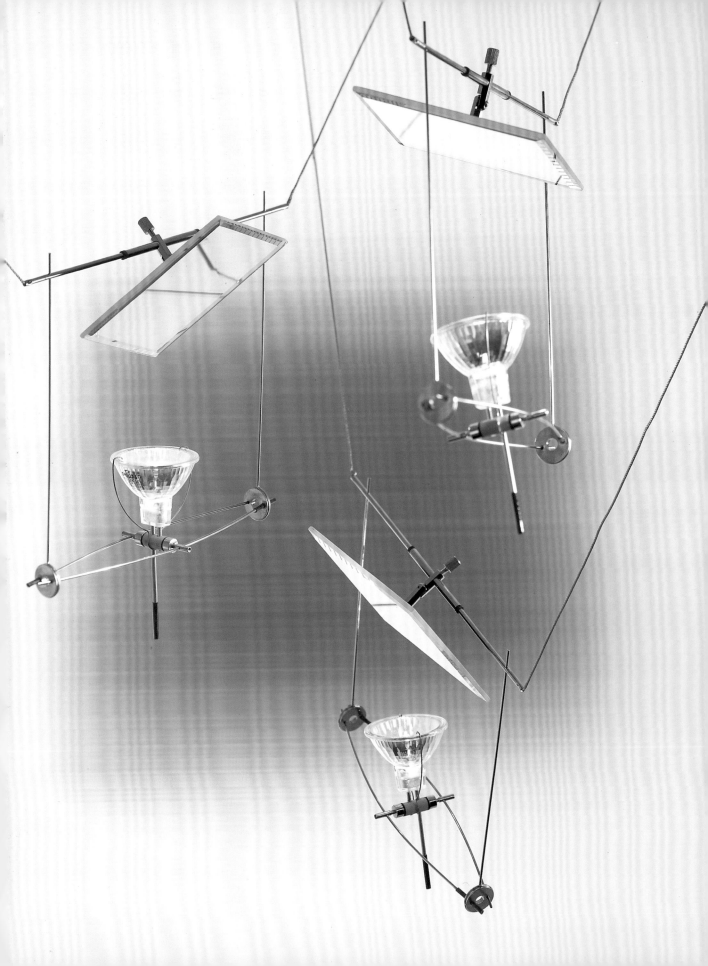

(Previous Spread)
Tableaux Chinois, 1989.
Water, mirrors, gold fish,
aluminum. Installation.

In 1989, Maurer was
approached to do a show
by the Fondation Cartier
pour l'Art Moderne in
France. He created what
he termed "free works"—
works freed from the
boundaries of product
design—many of which
used water to evoke
fascinating reflections
created by chance.

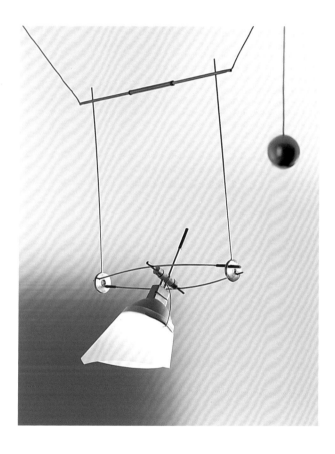

**YaYaHo, Element 2 with
mirror**, 1984. Porcelain,
glass, plastic, metal.

YaYaHo, Element 77,
1984. Porcelain, glass,
plastic, metal.

Pablo Picasso said this during an
interview for *Cahiers d'Art* in 1935.
I am not trying to equate my father's
work or way of creating with this
giant, or even name him as a major
influence. Chance—and the Internet—
merely led me to the quotation, and
chance is a concept of which Ingo
is very fond. I quote it here because
Picasso's answer seems of a piece
with Ingo's experience.

Inspiration is often a passing idea,
likely to get lost if you are not ready
to hang on to it, not tuned to the right
state of mind. As Picasso pointed out,
you need to be *receptive* to catch it.

When doing creative work, each individual has his or her own way of "tuning
in." Some need a disciplined environment, some need to go through certain
routines, while others invite inspiration
through exercise or relaxation.

For Ingo, inspiration is not to be found
in a quiet room sitting at a desk, or
while using drawing tools or computers,
or running in a park. His receptive state
of mind is instead triggered by sensu-
ous, physical well-being, including good
food, the occasional glass or two of
wine, and a free flow of subjects to talk
or think about—in short, a pleasurable,
relaxed environment. (Perhaps that
is why, wherever he goes in the world,
the restaurant napkin is his favorite
sketching medium; the resulting draw-
ings have become one of his trade-
marks.) Ingo's first lamp, *Bulb* (1966),
whose origins have been told many
times, is a good example of a design
derived from this particular mood.

Stress or tension resulting from the pressure to finish a project, or from the excitement of being confronted with a challenging offer in a conversation, also plays a crucial role in leading Ingo into a receptive state of mind. He says such demanding situations "make me amenable" to working.

After forty years of creative work in lighting design, Ingo is adept at seizing ideas and realizing their potential. In his case, the ability to draw on inspiration is necessary not only to ensure the success of an upcoming solo exhibition or of a new design for a client or manufacturer, but also to meet his company's monthly payroll.

Being both designer and producer gives Ingo ample freedom to make things look exactly the way he wants them to. The double role, however, also entails great responsibility. It was not a sense of self-assurance that led him to this mode of working, but rather his uncertainty regarding his own ideas and his strong dislike of giving in to clients' demands—the infamous "Yes, we love it, but could you do it in green?"

Apart from being tuned in to inspiration, one must also maintain an open mind in order to judge if an idea is worthy of consideration for product design, if it is feasible to produce and market. Without this receptive attitude, good ideas slip by unnoticed, while others are talked about then discarded right away because they are deemed uninteresting, impractical, or unappealing to potential customers.

Blushing Zettel'z, 2005.
Imprinted Japanese paper, stainless steel, glass.

A Chinese porcelain figure photographed for the images on *Blushing Zettel'z*.

Blushing Zettel'z (detail).

Don Quixote, 1989. Steel,
aluminum, flexible plastic.

An expression of myself.

Some of the most daring and acclaimed designs—not only by Ingo—were first welcomed by shocked looks that said, "We can't do that. It's embarrassing, absurd." "Ingo," an American friend once said, "has no fears of crossing boundaries."

In cultural fields, at least in Germany, people often worry about making mistakes when asked to propose their ideas or judge another's proposal. An American musician conducting workshops here pointed this out to me many years ago, and I think it is also true for other fields. When broaching a new idea, you can run the risk of appearing ignorant or tacky. It takes a measure of courage to plead an idea that at first seems cheesy or flat, but more than that, you need the freedom to think and to say, "This is so unusual that it may be startling, but it's good, it's right." In the business of furniture and lighting design, one that is certainly more commercial than the art scene, there is also the constant fear of doing something too shocking. To shock, you need to enjoy being a provocateur, which Ingo unmistakably does.

A long and fruitful career in creative work, like Ingo's, is one way to achieve this independence of thought. A big ego also helps, but Ingo claims he has never truly felt self-assured. Lack of formal training in your chosen field is another, albeit unorthodox, route to this independence, and here we home in on one of the "open" secrets of Ingo's work. His apprenticeship was in typography, not industrial design, and his early work was in graphic design.

In formal training, students are taught
to do things "right": They learn proven
approaches and appropriate techniques. They are taught to distinguish
between "good" and 'bad," and are,
depending on the Zeitgeist, pushed
toward the trends championed by
their teachers. Thus, formal education
is also the process of unlearning how
to follow one's ideas spontaneously,
which is, as Ingo would put it, a form
of brainwashing.[2]

With no formal education in industrial
design, Ingo's approach was, as a
matter of course, based on intuition.
When it comes to providing a rational
explanation, however, intuition is
perhaps as difficult a subject as inspiration. Both arise independently of
our predictions, let alone our control.
It is a question of temperament, and
whether you believe intuition and
inspiration grow within the mind, or
are instead bestowed by some super-
natural being, depends on your
Weltanschauung—your worldview.

Intuition is closely related to emotion,
and emotion is a vital component
of Ingo's work as well as his life. His
products and one-of-a-kind works
are not meant to be purely functional
or blend completely into a specific
environment. They should have a personality of their own, convey emotion,
and conjure it in those who see and
use them. As Ingo said in a 2003
interview, "A thing shouldn't stand
there like a lump of concrete, like a
monument for eternity. We are suc-
cessful when we manage to strike
a chord of feeling in people."

Nevertheless, Ingo's designs for serial production often leave room for users to express their feelings and ideas in the final form of the lamp—they are not pure statements of his ego. Ingo does not want to impose his ideas on the users of his lamps, and hopes they will bring their own imaginations to bear in completing them. Several products best demonstrate this approach: *YaYaHo*, *Zettel'z*, *Don Quixote*, the simple *Willy Dilly*, and the *Birds* family. When setting them up, users must make decisions regarding their forms. In this way, the lamps transmit the spark of inspiration that went into their design.

The emotions expressed in many of his works are positive and cheerful, if sometimes a little creepy (plastic rats and other little monsters are recurring elements). Here they diverge from works of art, which occasionally make use of shock in order to provoke feelings of sadness, fear, or even disgust. When asked, however, if what he is making is art or design—a question that often pops up in interviews— Ingo is always happy to allow his interviewers to decide for themselves.

In describing the work of other designers, he often mentions the absence of "a person behind the design"— in other words, an object's lack of emotion. Without question, Ingo's unabashedly emotional approach to design has won him both avid fans and determined detractors.

The lack of formal training, that knowledge passed from teacher to student, also results in a certain level of naïveté. The naïve mind is not inhibited by acquired paths of thinking, by "dos" and "don'ts," or by the knowledge that something has already been made by so-and-so. It is free to move and follow images and inspirations as they come, free to indulge in dreams that seem unrealistic to others. Ingo has said that, when he first participated in major trade fairs in the late 1960s, he did not know much about the Castiglioni brothers or other designers of the preceding generation. This situation has changed a great deal because he has long tried to absorb as much information about the field as possible.

At a certain point in his career, writers started to call Ingo a "magician of light,"[3] an appellation referenced by the title of Ingo's exhibition at Cooper-Hewitt. Real magic, as opposed to that produced by sleight of hand, cannot exist without some naïveté. Contemporary magicians produce a lot of stunning effects on stage, but, as the adults (and many of the children) in the audience know, they all rely on tricks and hidden mechanisms. Otherwise, what they present would simply be too frightening. Perhaps the magicians of old could, after much training, conjure objects and make the incredible happen, and lead those bereft of naïveté to search for explanations. Nevertheless, today, many rationally thinking people, trained in the sciences, still cherish the notion that magic exists. This belief first arises during childhood, before our formal education begins, before we are

Wiz Wiz Wizzard, 2005. Ribbon cable, circuit boards, LED, glass, metal, plastic. Prototype.

The ribbon cable also acts as a structural element. Several lighting elements using both LED and low-voltage halogen light sources, some equipped with mirrors, can be attached anywhere along the ribbon. Among the elements is a module for the display of short messages from mobile phones. *Wiz Wiz Wizzard* was the first lighting system with one cable presented worldwide.

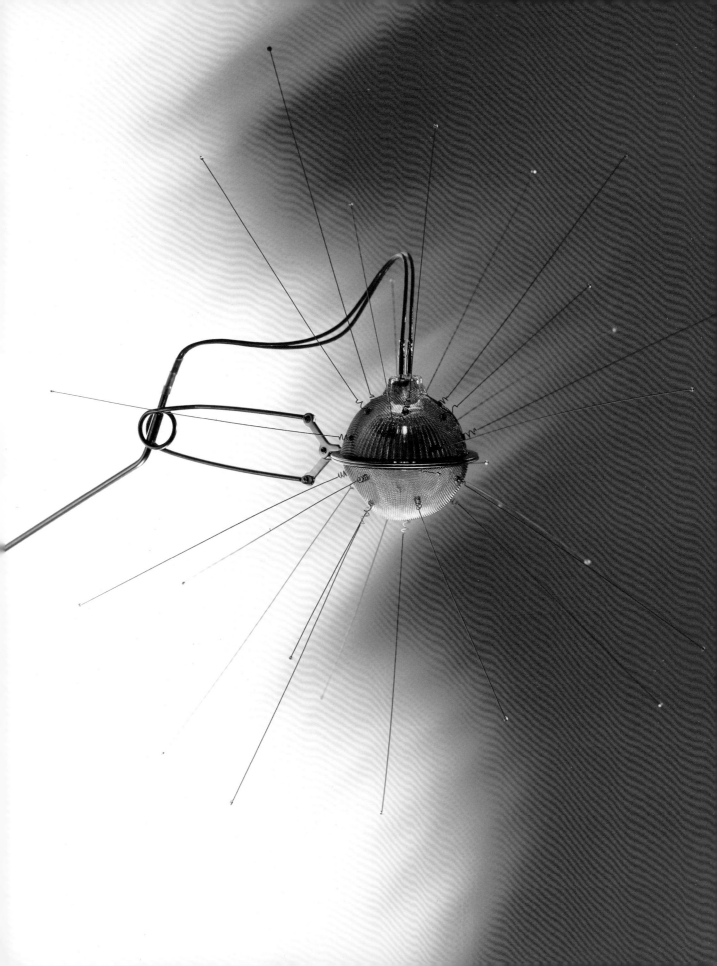

Mozzkito, 1996.
Metal, rubber.

Mozzkito sketch, 1996.
Pen on paper.

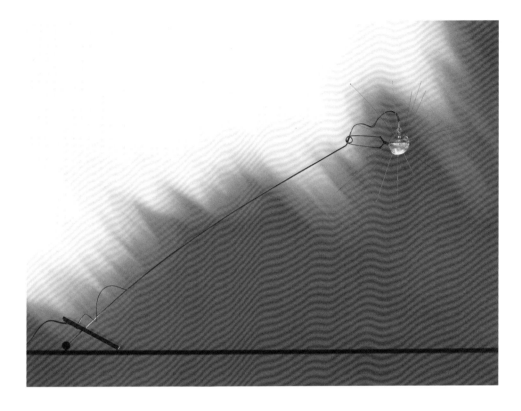

blinkered by the impossibilities of the modern world. It is this attitude, this state of mind, that Ingo manages to keep alive, that allows him to open himself to inspiration, the fruits of which enchant countless visitors at trade fairs and exhibitions.

Despite his background, Ingo does not disapprove of formal training in the field of design; nor does he underestimate the benefits of acquiring skills and exploring design-world issues. Without such skills, designers would not be able to manufacture serial products. For many years, Ingo has been working with an evolving and expanding team of designers, architects, and engineers. He has never been reluctant to point out the importance of this collaboration, one that has been aided by the extensive formal skills of his team members, as well as by the many technical innovations that find their way into his work. Still, it is interesting to speculate whether Ingo would have done things differently had he gone to a design school.

So where do Ingo's inspirations come from? One element, mentioned in Picasso's answer, is the scrap of paper— an utterly ordinary object we encounter every day. We also have the bulb, the tea strainer, workshop clamps, circuit boards, notes on paper. Ingo has managed to view ordinary objects with his extraordinary eyes, uncovering their beauty and finding stimulation in them. It is his open mind and freedom of thought that enable this perception, and Ingo is, by no means, the first designer to reinvent the ordinary.

OLED object, 2006.
White organic LEDs, plastic, metal.

In products like *Mozzkito* and *Don Quixote*, the inspirational trigger for an object is not always closely bound to its final form. Last summer, I accompanied my father to China for a few days. For once, our schedule was not too busy, and a European friend showed us around. At a market, we saw crickets for sale in tiny, round bamboo cages attached to each other like a large bunch of grapes. Later in the year, with some of his team members, Ingo started to experiment with small, cubical cages made of thin metal wire, stacking them in different ways. These cricket cages morphed into the suspended object *A Memory from Shanghai - or was it Cairo?* and two smaller table lamps, with plastic creatures in some of the cages.

While the Chinese crickets in their cages cannot really be considered "natural"—the way pets live in most countries is quite unnatural—nature is certainly one source of Ingo's inspiration, though perhaps less pronounced than the spider's web was for Picasso. Water, wind, and all permutations of natural light and its reflection play a crucial role in Ingo's work. Perhaps these influences derive from his youth on an island in Lake Constance, or maybe from an innate aesthetic sensibility.

Reflections of light on water are very difficult to realize in designs for serial production, and it was not until 1989, when the Fondation Cartier pour l'art contemporain offered him a solo exhibition of non-product objects in Jouy-en-Jousas, near Paris, that Ingo was

LED wedding dresses,
2002. Designers: Ingo
Maurer with Janet Hansen.
Cloth, LED, flexible circuit
boards. One-off.

able to create works highlighting
this element. A first version of
Tableaux Chinois, in which live fish
trigger the movement of water and
swimming mirrors cast a multitude
of reflections, was part of that exhibition. Later, in large commissioned
works like *Earthbound - Unbound* for
the Toronto International Airport
and the *Water Column* (2005) for a
hotel in Maastricht, the Netherlands,
he had the chance to use water again;
he was also able to harness wind
for Issey Miyake's London showroom
in 1999. The movement of the light-
weight leaves and their reflections
epitomize the yearning for lightness
and transitoriness expressed in
many of Ingo's works.

Are we any closer to pinpointing
the source of Ingo's inspiration? Is
he merely a vessel for transporting
the various aesthetic impressions I
have described? After all, even if we
can detect and examine some of its
facets, inspiration ultimately remains
indefinable. Viewing it as a gift of
the Christian Holy Spirit or the Greek
Muses, many centuries of European
thought have assigned a divine prove-
nance to artistic inspiration. I do not
think Ingo has paid deep attention
to the question of where his inspiration stems from—whether from a
divine being or the subconscious—
but I know he believes in light's unde-
niably spiritual quality, and considers
it the friendly ghost that surrounds
us. Lighting has a great impact not
only on our feelings and well-being,
but also on our receptivity to inspiration—something that we all seek.

Les Rêves des Diamants, exhibition design for Chanel, 2002. Gold dust, diamonds, air compressor.

Gold dust is flung in the air in rhythmic intervals, then slowly sinks down in the light of the spotlights. The object has a height of approximately 1.5 meters. The first installation was shown at the exhibition *Lumière Hasard Réflection* at the Fondation Cartier pour l'Art Moderne under the title *Le Dust de Cartier*.

Translated from the German by Charles Worthen

1 "Conversation avec Picasso," in *Cahiers d'Art*, vol. 10, no. 10, 1935; translated in Alfred H. Barr, Jr., *Picasso: Fifty Years of His Art* (New York: Museum of Modern Art, 1946).

2 Ingo said that his apprenticeship as typographer, chosen out of necessity at age fifteen, was important for his later career because working with letter cases and sizes, typefaces, and the spacing between words gave him vital training in recognizing details.

3 Ingo has also many times been called a "poet of light" in the press.

Plastic rat with mask, for
*A Memory from Shanghai,
or was it Cairo?*

Ingo Maurer working on
*A Memory from Shanghai,
or was it Cairo?*, 2007.

Study for A Memory from Shanghai, or was it Cairo? Gold-plated metal cages, plastic.

A Memory from Shanghai, or was it Cairo sketch, 2007. Pen on paper.

(Next spread)
Seven Rats, 2007. Prototype for a table lamp. Gold-plated metal cages, brass, plastic.

Moon over Cuba, 2007. Prototype for a table lamp. Gold-plated metal cages, brass, plastic. Limited edition.

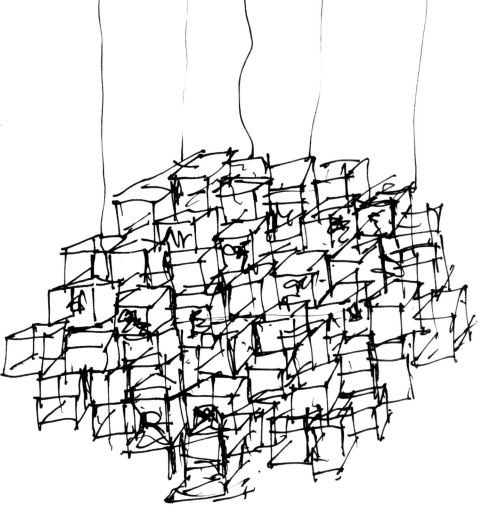

Memories of Shanghai or was it Cairo?

Orgia d'Oro, 1995.
Gold-plated metal, plastic,
Plexiglas, brass. One-off.

HOT.HOT, 2006.
Metal, glass lenses.

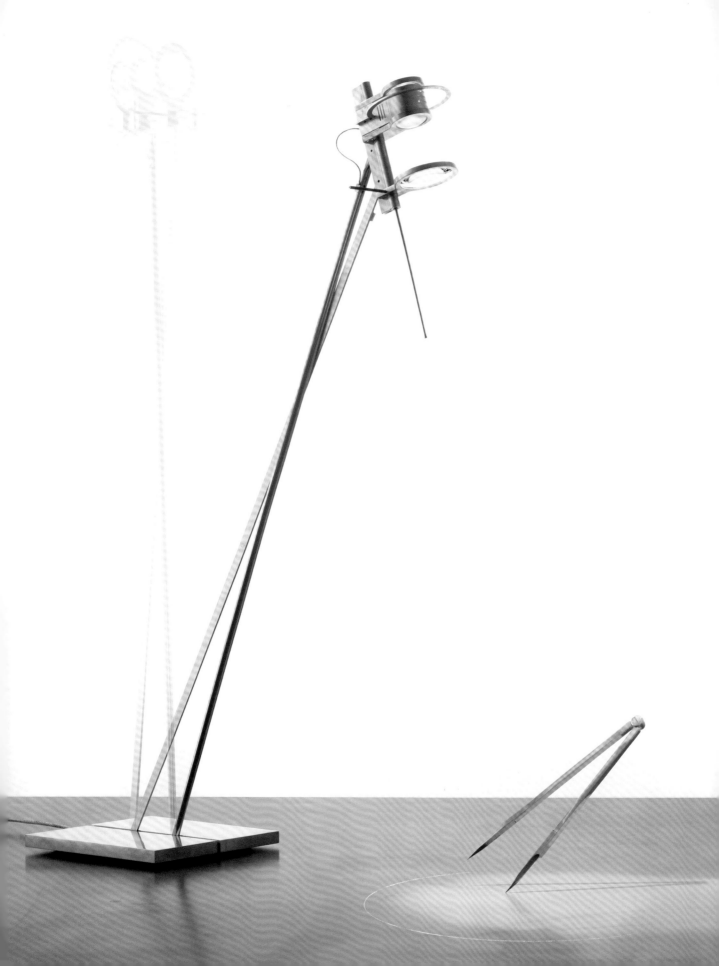

**A Friendly Intrusion
from Outer Space**,
2006. Fiberglass, plastic,
metal, polished alumnium.
Installed in the Atomium,
Brussels, Belgium, built
in 1958 and renovated in
2006. Custom-made object.

101

Wafer, 2006. Installed in the Atomium, Brussels, Belgium. Steel, aluminum.

YUU 200, 2006. Installed in the Atomium, Brussels, Belgium. Fiberglass, aluminum, steel.

a-Tool, 2003. Designer: Christoph Matthias. Aluminum, stainless steel, plastic.

A device inside the grip renders the light head freely adjustable within the suspension points.

(Next spread)
Campari Light, 2002. Designer: Raffaele Celentano. Campari Soda bottles, plastic, metal.

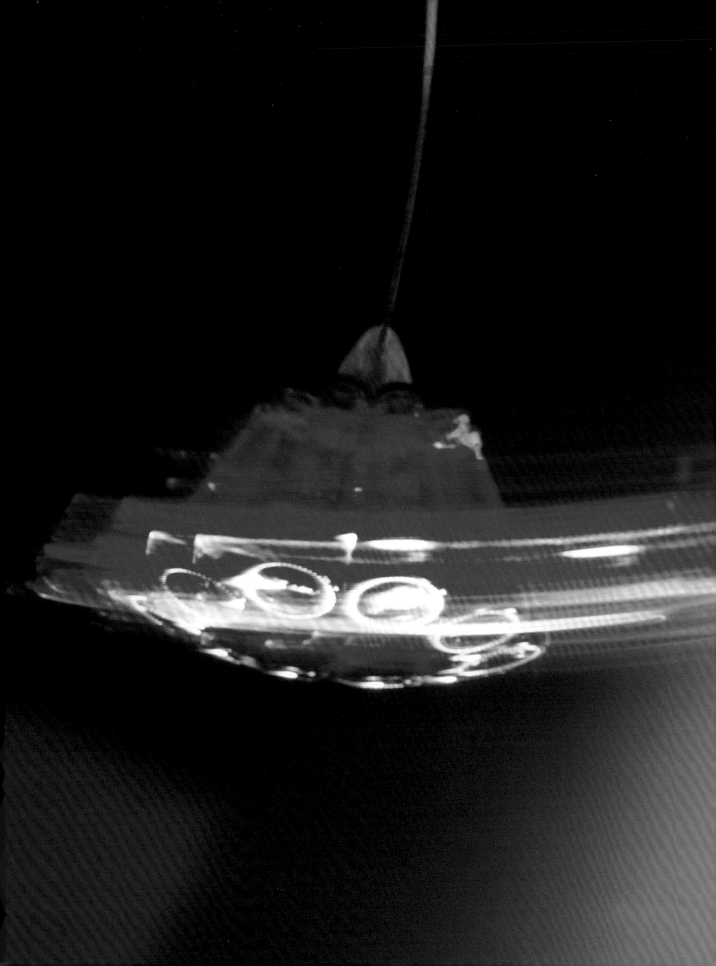

(Opposite)
Bitter Lemon, 2001.
Juicy Salif Juicer by
Philippe Starck, 1990,
with shade made of
optical film, metal, and
plastic. Prototype.

According to Maurer,
Horny Philippe and *Bitter
Lemon* are his response to
some of friend Philippe
Starck's work.

Horny Philippe sketch,
1998.

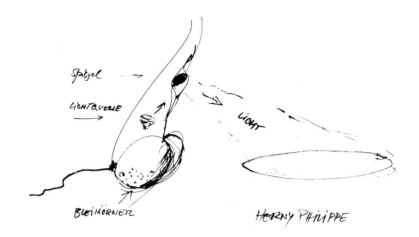

**Hana in a nude costume
with a prototype of
Horny Philippe**. In the
background, Ingo Maurer
with a Philippe Starck
mask. From an installa-
tion/performance for a
product presentation dur-
ing the Cologne Furniture
Fair, 1998.

(Previous spread)
Pierre ou Paul, 1996.
Aluminum, stainless steel.

Delirium Yum, 2006.
Designers: Ingo Maurer
with Sebastian Hepting.
Glass, metal, Corian,
aluminum, plastic.

Delirium Yum sketch,
2005. Pen on paper.

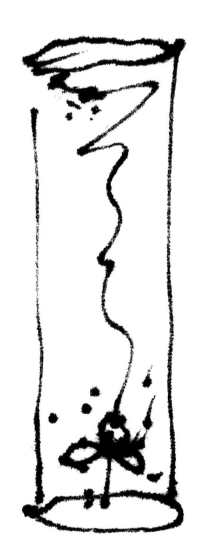

**Installation for a private
residence in Switzerland**,
2005. Polished aluminum
pendulum, recessed light
installation forming the
I-Ching symbols in the floor.
Photo print as triptych.

**Water wall with moving
nude figures, installation
for a private residence
in Switzerland**, 2005.
Acrylic, plastic, water,
air compressor.

Water wall (detail).

117

(Opposite)
**Big Dish suspension
lamps in the
Kruisherenhotel**,
Maastricht, the
Netherlands, 2005.
Fiberglass, metal, light
head with CMY color
mixing system. Custom-
made suspension.

118

The egg is 3 meters in height
and sways a little
as if it would fall.

**Proposal for an entrance
hall in New York**, photo-
mounting, 2006.

LED Table and custom-made supension, 2003.
LED Table: laminated safety glass, metal, 278 LEDs per panel; suspension: aluminum, metal.

120

Think of fireflies in a garden.

122

LED Bench, 2002.
Laminated safety glass,
288 LEDs. Limited edition.

LED Table, 2007 version,
with special version of
Schlitz, 2007. LED table:
laminated safety glass;
Schlitz (length approx. 5
meters): fiberglass, metal.
Limited edition.

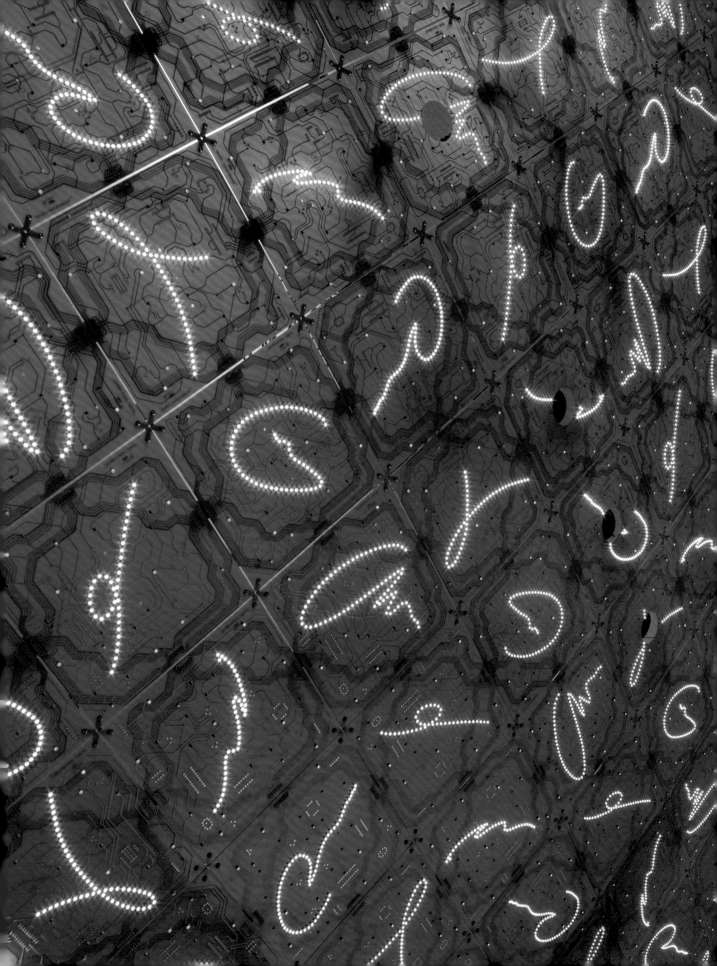

(Previous spread)
One Thousand and One Lights. One-off.

The color and brightness of the RGB-LEDs can be adjusted and programmed.

One Thousand and One Lights, 2006. Circuit boards, RGB-LEDs, metal.

LED Paravent, 2007. Circuit boards, RGB-LEDs, metal. One-off.

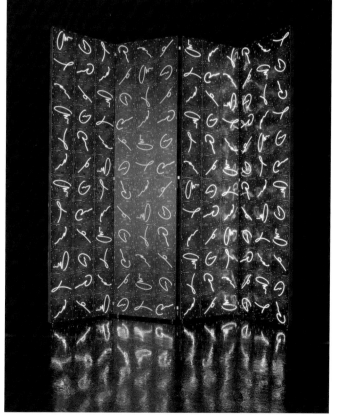

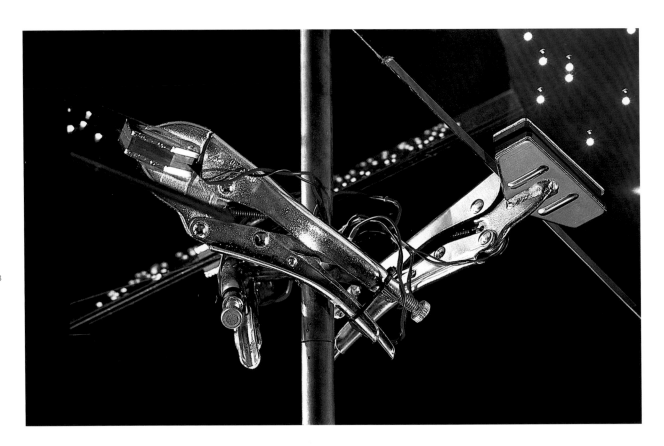

Stardust (detail).

Stardust, 2000. Safety
glass with LEDs, metal,
aluminum. Limited edition.

I HAVE BEEN DREAMING FOR A LONG TIME OF A WALLPAPER WHICH LIGHTS UP.

WE HAVE DONE IT!! SHOWN FOR THE FIRST TIME IN MILANO 2007. YOU CAN CHANGE PATTERN AND COLORS, SOFT OR STRONG JUST AS YOU FEEL.

LED Wallpaper, 2007.
Plastic film, white, red
and blue LEDs. Prototype.

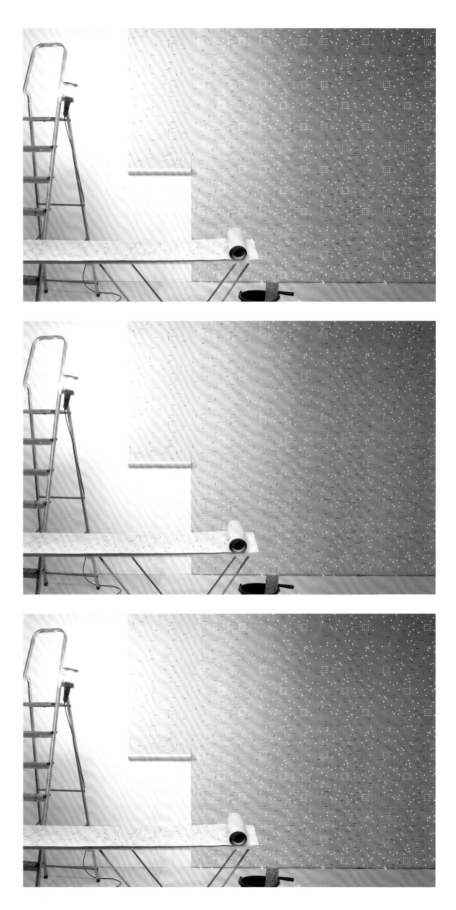

Lüster, 2003. Imprinted, molded glass, LEDs.

Sketches for Lüster, 2003. Pen on paper.

Fly, Candle, Fly!, 2000.
Designers: Ingo Maurer
with Georg Baldele. Wax
candle, suspension wire.

(Next spread)
**Installation with Fly,
Candle, Fly!** for an event
in Alhambra Theater, New
York, NY, 2000.

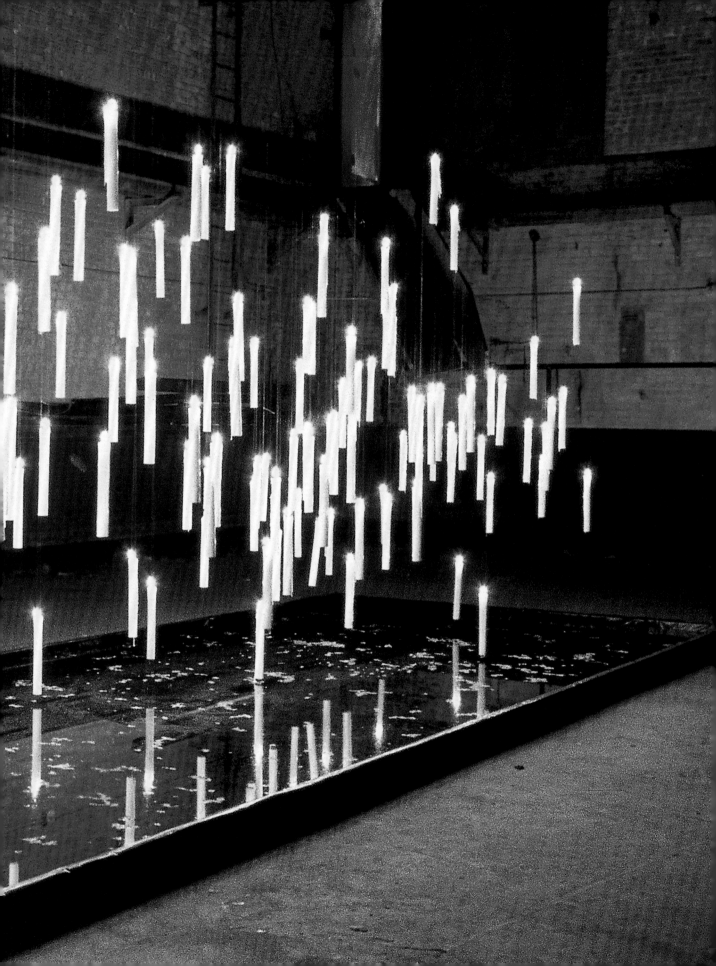

138

Photo for the presentation of TU-BEs (detail).

TU-BEs, 2007. Designers: Ingo Maurer in collaboration with Ron Arad. Metal, aluminum toothpaste tubes, LED and halogen light sources. Prototype for limited edition.

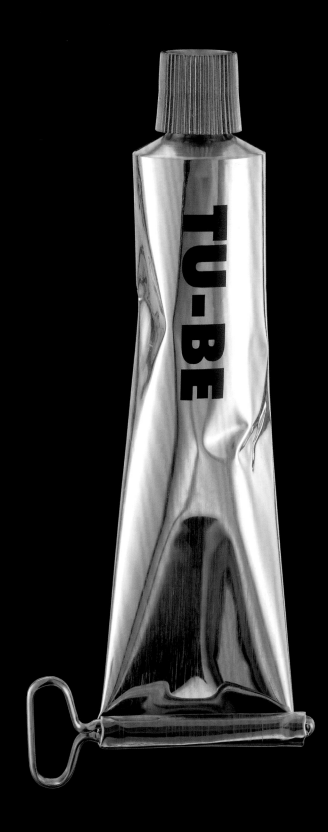

Abgefahren lighting object for the Rockhal concert hall, Luxembourg, 2007. Metal, plastic, wood, rubber; length: 15 meters. Object.

The essential part of the object is still recognizable as a car, blown up as if in the still of an explosion. Lights flash, and fog drifts out from the center, diffusing the light in an intriguing way. "Abgefahren" denotes "departed" in German; but in slang usage, it means "spacy" or "far out."

(Next spread)
Neon object for an entrance hall in a private residence (detail), London, England, 2007. Metal, aluminum, neon tubes, plastic. One-off.

First prototype of suspension Living Vegas, 2007. Metal, aluminum, neon tubes, plastic.

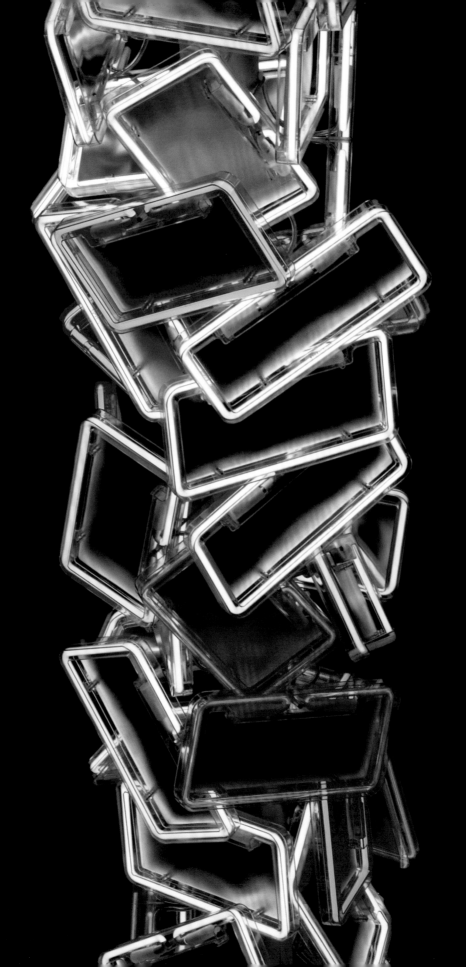

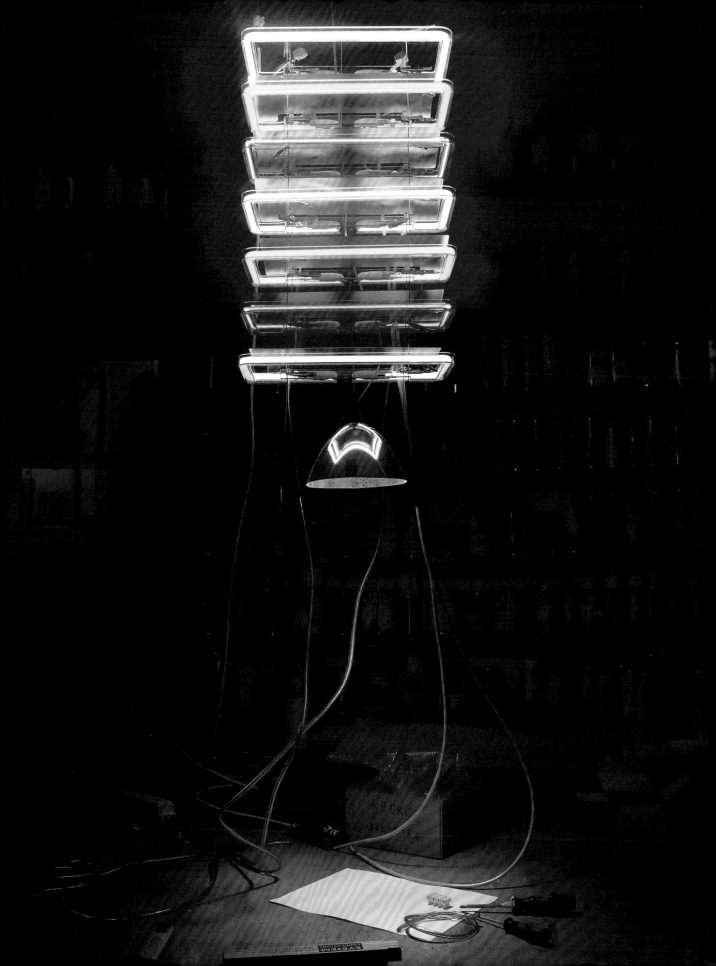

UNICEF Crystal Snowflake, 2005. Stainless steel, metal, crystal prisms; diameter: 7 meters. One-off.

Since 2005, during the end-of-year holiday season, Maurer's UNICEF Crystal Snowflake graces the intersection of Fifth Avenue and 57th Street in Manhattan. The snowflake is a three-dimensional, twelve-arm sculpture made of stainless steel, light, and more than 10,000 sparkling Baccarat crystals.

Provoking
Magic through
Collaboration

TROJAN SCHMID
from a series of interviews with
Ingo Maurer and members of the
Maurer Studio

THE MAURER MAGIC

Light, whether natural or artificial, shapes our world and makes it visible. We arrange our lives around light, yet most of us know little about it. As Benjamin Franklin noted in 1752, "I am much in the *Dark* about *Light*."[1] By contrast, Ingo Maurer's lights and lighting installations are not passive, functional objects, like most of the lighting we encounter on a daily basis. Instead, for Maurer, his studio "family," and anyone who views them, his lights have animate, almost sentient personalities, and the installations he designs enliven their surrounding space. Their active presence compels us to acknowledge their magical and transformative abilities and to celebrate light's ephemeral and illusory nature. As a member of the Maurer team observes, "Just as light merges with other elements in the natural environment, Ingo knows how to push borders when designing serial products, how to let the light intermingle with water, fire, air, and earth in a poetic way."

Most lighting is designed primarily for functionality in whatever "style" is prevalent at the time. However, few, if any, of Maurer's lights look alike; and they are defined less by "style" than by their distinctive materials, form, "personality," and the nature of the light they impart. Since the 1960s, Maurer has been among the first to take advantage of new technologies, whether embedding light in clothing, chairs, tables, and walls, or creating light in any physical forms that catch his imagination. Anyone viewing Maurer's work for the first time must give up all preconceived ideas of how artificial light should look or act. Beyond any functionality, Maurer's lighting regularly crosses from design into contemporary art, but without the elitism, affectation, or arrogance of the art world.

Both subtle and overt humor and, on occasion, sexuality are characteristics of a number of Maurer's works. From children's toys, rubber chicken's feet, and commercial tea strainers to small plastic copulating figures, Maurer finds inspiration and materials for his lights everywhere. He takes nothing seriously but the beauty of the materials and the nature, mood, and atmosphere of the resulting light. Once that is achieved to his satisfaction, he immediately moves on to the next idea that captures his imagination.

MAURER'S WORKING "FAMILY"

Maurer began in Munich in 1966 with only five staff members. Today, more than sixty people work in the company. Although most members of the

(Previous spread)
Ingo Maurer in 2005.

(This spread)
Symphonia Silenziosa, 1999. Installation for an Issey Miyake fashion show in Paris, France.

Symphonia Silenziosa sketch. Pen on paper.

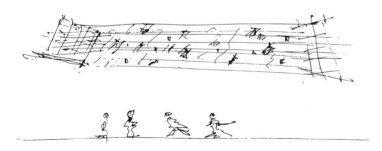

design team joined thinking their tenure would only last a few years, several have remained for much longer. As Maurer acknowledges, "I work with wonderful people and I couldn't do anything without them. It is like a great family. Some of my designers have been there a long time—perhaps too long. They should fly out and do their own things. In many ways, I am younger in my mind than they." Maurer's continuing passion for his work and for those with whom he works is evident in his gestures, words, and actions. One of Maurer's close collaborators remembers the time the two of them lay on the floor, "like children," in order to look at the light overhead.

Maurer notes, "Some of my design staff are not designers, but have enormous understanding and a huge spectrum of sensibilities and knowledge. All of the people in my studio are skilled and necessary in their own way. It is important that they be there for major projects, or I would drive the clients crazy. Jenny Lau, my wife, is my *éminence grise* and keeps me happy and sane." A unique aspect of being part of the Maurer team is that the designer, as a matter of course, always insists that the contributions of his "collaborators" (the term he uses to identify members of Ingo Maurer GmbH) be acknowledged. In this, he is quite different from most other artists and designers. This in turn engenders deep loyalty among those who work with him. As one of the design and project development team notes, "Not only is Ingo a creative, dynamic force in his own right, he is a

person with compassion and heart.
It has been an honor and a pleasure
working together with him."

A large part of the continuous, seemingly endless creativity reflected in
Maurer's work can be attributed
to these unusually close relationships.
Another collaborator joined Ingo
Maurer GmbH in 1998 because, as he
describes it, he was not interested in
working on only one part of a design,
but wanted to be able to "jump in and
tackle problems as they arise, to experiment and improvise—to exercise ini-
tiative and yet work as part of a team."
The area of the studio where the design
and development team works is filled
with prototypes, models, paper, metal,
wire, and various materials piled on
desks and shelves and hanging from
the ceiling. Maurer does not have an
office—not even a proper desk—but
manages the creative process by walk-
ing around, stopping to discuss and
comment on every work in every stage
of completion.

Like an artist, Maurer pushes materials
beyond their understood boundaries, and
he surrounds himself with people that
are highly skilled in many diverse areas.
According to Maurer, "Anyone who
works for me has to be good with his or
her hands—one guy told me he could
take tractors apart; another did his the-
sis on an airship device for conducting
scientific research on trees and treetops.
It is wonderful to have all these talented
individuals, and each one I sense differently, which is my greatest pleasure. I
pick certain people for the challenges
for which I know they are best suited."

The workshop for paper
shades at Ingo Maurer
GmbH, 2002.

i am a slave! of myself and others...

and of my many ideas!

The *MaMo Nouchies*
development room at Ingo
Maurer GmbH, 1996.

Like Maurer, his designers make up
the rules as they work, rather than
following any prescribed laws on how
materials or technology should be
used. Maurer often quotes Einstein's
statement that "imagination is more
important than knowledge." As he
notes, "I do not like to analyze how
things come about. I am afraid of
becoming too conscious and one day
looking over my own shoulder, watching myself working. Sometimes there
is a 'click' that starts things off, and
I like the joy of progressing from idea
to result." The team members each
have their individual ways of working,
and they are not all alike. As one member says, "We complement each other,
and nobody has to adapt to an 'Ingo-
Maurer-GmbH style' when starting to
work here. This 'style' does not exist."

Most of Maurer's work derives from
inspirations he gets daily from the
world around him, and he only accepts
commissions that are a challenge,
insisting that he have complete control
over the look, arrangement, and techniques used to realize the final product.
Usually, Maurer first imagines the kind
and mood of light he wants to achieve
and the needs of his client. Sometimes
he is inspired by an unusual material
or object he has seen. Then he works
with his designers to determine what
materials and technology are needed to
achieve that result. "Work begins with
an idea I have or a mood I want to create. I then go to people who I think can
realize that idea, and tell them what I
have in mind—a feeling of what I want
to create, perhaps through a sketch on
paper or a napkin. We discuss it so that

89 GRAND ST.
N.Y.C.
N.Y.
CHANGED
MY LIFE
I.M.

they become really involved, and show me how they might solve the problem or meet the challenge I have set. Then I let them go. Sometimes the result is different from what I imagined or like, but I am open to the designers' fighting for their ideas. The fun is the dialogue of working together to find the right solution. There are these moments when this happens, when we all shout "We've got it!" that are so wonderful. There is an enormous sense of intimacy among all of us—sharing the success together."

Many individual works, such as the *YaYaHo* and *MaMo Nouchies*, involve new and unique uses of materials. The lighting ideas usually derive from Maurer, and the solutions are achieved through communication among members of the studio using rough sketches, exploratory models, gestures, and frank discussion. Many different materials are tested until one is found that "feels right." Designing is always a balancing act to find the right technique, the right materials, the right form and clarity, which combine together to form the integrated whole. As one of the designers who worked for Maurer from 1986 to 1996 describes, "You often find yourself running up blind alleys; finding the center of the maze is a laborious business, and sometimes you get completely lost, or you suddenly realize that the center is not actually there. That is one of the big dangers in design."[2]

Close collaboration among the company's departments (management, sales, design, production, packing, and shipping) is an integral part of every

153

work. Maurer refers to his whole company as a "garden, full of all kinds of flowers: some smell delicious, others are breathtaking." For one collaborator, Maurer's studio "redefines collaboration" so that everyone is "encouraged to create new work, suggest new possibilities, explore ideas, and figure out different ways to solve the challenges in Maurer's designs." As he further observes, "Teamwork in the studio means constantly having interesting project. I stay because of the mixture of work, the continual surprises, the variety of countries where our work is installed.... Ingo encourages us to seek our own solutions, but many cannot be realized alone. The result is better when you let it out in the open and other people get involved."

Maurer adds, "The 'we' is crucial to our work. Sometimes our group becomes too ingrown and constipated, or become *culo pesante* (an Italian idiom which literally means 'heavy ass') in the brain. Then it is time to bring in someone new, to look at the work fresh, and propose different answers. I like to invite all kinds of people from all walks of life to the studio to react to the works and provoke our thinking in a new way. A street bum, for example, brings a completely different perspective and way of looking and thinking about a work. But openness to too many ideas can also be difficult." Maurer and his team work at an astonishing rate, designing many international projects and new lights in a single year. A team member observes, "To work with Ingo means to be in permanent motion, to never

Ingo Maurer showroom in Soho, New York, NY, 2001.

pause because you are out of breath. It means curiosity and emotion, intuition and sensuality."

Each of Maurer's designs is unique in terms of the time it takes from concept to completion. The *YaYaHo* lighting system took almost four years from conception to completion. Maurer and his team expected work on the *MaMo Nouchies* series to take three months; instead, it took three years. The design process began with an examination of traditional textile dyeing techniques adapted to Japanese paper, the idea of a former team member who had experimented with textile and paper. Maurer recalls, "When I saw the material and designs for the first time, my spirit soared, and my imagination ran wild with the possibilities. Immediately, there were so many ideas for using this technique that the most difficult thing was deciding which of them to choose from." To allow for full concentration, and to prevent anyone from plagiarizing the technique before it was perfected, two senior members of the team spent over a year working in a secluded part of the studio, known as "the blue room," that only Maurer was allowed to enter. "After a year, we opened the space for everyone and showed them the ten to fifteen models we had made."

In the last few years, Maurer and his professional "family" have designed and developed a number of site-specific installations. Many of them are enormous in scale; all of them are spectacular and unpredictable, for the viewers as well as for the participants. One team member swam in a fountain for a temporary event: "I wore a diving suit and luminous ivy, I lit torches that burned underwater and imitated the chirping of crickets. That's not what you call a monotonous working routine. First and foremost, the collaboration is incredibly exciting, you never get stuck in a rut."

Maurer keeps meticulous records of his completed works. He shares his new designs at design fairs, such as the annual fair in Milan, and publishes beautiful, full-color catalogues of his newest objects and installations. These publications are written and produced at the same rapid pace as the works themselves. According to a member of his publications and sales department, "Mostly the deadlines are very tight, the texts have to be finalized really fast. When Ingo is in Munich, many of my colleagues need to talk to him to clarify issues that have come up in the meantime. He has hardly any time to pause. Then he hurries to my desk, sits down, folds his arms behind his neck, and within seconds he is completely concentrated on the task and coming up with concepts. Full of ideas, he outlines the text so fast that it is hard to follow taking notes. And that is exactly what I like about him: he is always devoted to his work, his company, and his employees with his whole mind, and he does that in an emotional, joyful, and human way."

Maurer's creations are inspired by genius, generated out of passionate collaboration, and, ultimately, entirely unique. Each of Maurer's works provokes viewers and users to bring their individual experiences, thoughts, and dreams to "complete" them. This in turn forges an emotional bond beyond any usual relationship with inanimate objects. The results are surprising, whimsical, varied, and reflect an inimitable form of magic. During the last forty years, Maurer has created more than 150 lights and lighting installations. And he has no intention of stopping anytime soon.

1   Quoted in Cadwallader Colden, 23 April 1752, *The Papers of Benjamin Franklin*, vol. 4 (New Haven: Yale University Press, 1961), p. 299.
2   Quoted in *Ingo Maurer: Making Light*, edited by Helmut Bauer (Munich: Nazraeli Press, 1992), p. 121.

ACKNOWLEDGMENTS

Cooper-Hewitt, National Design Museum would like to thank the following individuals and organizations, listed in no particular order, for their invaluable help and cooperation during the preparation of the *Provoking Magic: Lighting of Ingo Maurer* exhibition and book.

The entire staff of Ingo Maurer GmbH

At Cooper-Hewitt: Communications and Marketing: William Berry, Jennifer Northrop, Laurie Olivieri; Curatorial: Matilda McQuaid, Alicia Arroyo; Development/External Affairs: Debbie Ahn, Caroline Baumann, Lauren Gray; Exhibitions: Matthew O'Connor, Mathew Weaver; Registrar: Melanie Fox, Steven Langehough, Wendy Rogers

Smithsonian Institution: Steve Roth, Janice Slivko

Tsang Seymour Design: Patrick Seymour, Susan Brzozowski, Michael Brenner

Tim Nissen
Mary Ann Hoag
AKF Engineering
Patriot Electric
Small Corp.

For more information on the Museum and the exhibition, visit Cooper-Hewitt's Web site, www.cooperhewitt.org.

PHOTOGRAPHIC CREDITS

Cooper-Hewitt, National Design Museum is grateful to Ingo Maurer GmbH and other organizations and individuals for their permission to reproduce images in this book. Every effort has been made to trace and contact the copyright holders of the images reproduced; any errors or omissions shall be corrected in subsequent editions. All images refer to page numbers unless otherwise stated.

All photos are by Tom Vack, © Ingo Maurer GmbH, except the following:

Title page: Hans Buttermilch

Kim Hastreiter
pp. 10–11: Hagen Sczech
p. 16: Thomas Dix
p. 17: Donato di Bello, Domus

Julie Iovine
p. 39: Friedrich Busam
pp. 41, 43 (top), 45: Markus Tollhopf
p. 43 (bottom): Hagen Sczech
pp. 58–59: Thomas Dix, courtesy of Vitra Design Museum
p. 60: Hans Buttermilch
p. 63: Nomi Baumgartl

Claude Maurer
p. 66: Rafael Vargas
p. 67: Georges Meguerditchian
p. 72: Christof Piepenstock
p. 86: Hagen Sczech
p. 87: Jean-François Gaté/Elle Décoration

p. 108: Markus Tollhopf

p. 118: photo montage, © Ingo Maurer GmbH

p. 119: Nacasa & Partners

pp. 128–29: Markus Tollhopf

pp. 134–35: Peter Cook

pp. 136–37: Barbara Alper
p. 140 (bottom): Stefan Braun

pp. 142–43: Hagen Sczech

p. 144: Jonathan B. Ragle

Trojan Schmid
p. 146: Fico
p. 150: Hagen Sczech
p. 151: Markus Tollhopf
p. 152: Antoine Bootz
p. 154: Jonathan B. Ragle

PROVOKING MAGIC
Lighting of Ingo Maurer
© 2007 Smithsonian Institution

Published by
Cooper-Hewitt, National Design Museum
Smithsonian Institution
2 East 91st Street
New York, NY 10128, USA
www.cooperhewitt.org

Published on the occasion of the exhibition
Provoking Magic: Lighting of Ingo Maurer
at Cooper-Hewitt, National Design Museum,
Smithsonian Institution,
September 14, 2007–January 27, 2008.

Provoking Magic: Lighting of Ingo Maurer is made
possible by **Bloomberg**.

This publication is made possible in part by
The Andrew W. Mellon Foundation.

Distributed to the trade worldwide by
Assouline Publishing
601 West 26th Street, 18th floor
New York, NY 10001, USA
www.assouline.com

All rights reserved. No part of this book may
be reproduced in any form or by any electronic
or mechanical means, including information storage
and retrieval systems, without permission in
writing from the publisher, except by a reviewer
who may quote brief passages in a review.

First edition: September 2007

ISBN: 0-910503-94-X (book)
ISBN: 0-910503-93-1 (case)
Library of Congress CIP data available
from the publisher.

Museum Editor: Chul R. Kim, Head of Publications
Design: Tsang Seymour Design, Inc.
Printed in China by Oceanic Graphic Printing.

Front cover:
L'Eclat Joyeux, 2005
White European and colored Chinese porcelain,
chopsticks, metal
One-off
Courtesy of Ingo Maurer, photo: Tom Vack

Back cover: L'Eclat Joyeux (detail)